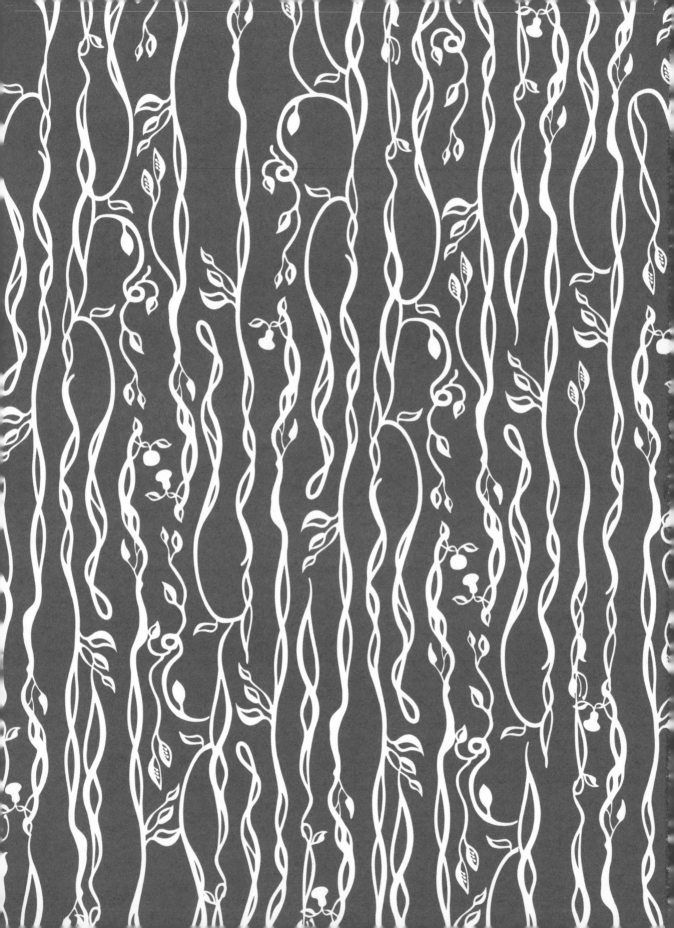

The Kitchen Orchard

The Kitchen Orchard

Fridge foraging
and simple
feasts

Natalia Conroy

EBURY PRESS

For Katya and Eric

CONTENTS

Introduction   12

Cooking notes   18

1 The Top Vegetable Drawer

PARSLEY, GARLIC, BASIL   22

Peppers, Parsley, Garlic   24

Carrots, Parsley, Honey   26

Chicken, Parsley, Green Beans   27

Swiss Chard, Parsley, Spinach   28

Chicken, Parsley, Carrot Soup   32

Fennel Broth, Parsley, Chicken   34

Lentils, Ramsons, Basil   36

Tomato, Parsley, Garlic   37

Chicken, Parsley, Breadcrumbs   38

Ham Hock, Parsley, Dandelion   41

Borlotti, Parsley, Bread Soup   47

Basil, Garlic, Pine Nuts 1   50

Basil, Garlic, Pine Nuts 2   51

Chickpeas, Garlic, Paprika   52

DILL, MINT   54

Aubergines, Mint, Raisins   56

Aubergines, Dill, Potatoes   58

Khobez, Mint, Lemon   59

Tomatoes, Dill, Sherry Vinegar   60

Kohlrabi, Mint, Smoked Paprika   62

Peas, Mint, Dill 63

Peas, Dill, Little Gem Lettuce 64

Courgettes, Mint, Ricotta 66

Honey, Dill, Mustard 69

Green Leaves, Dill, Radish 70

Lamb Chops, Mint, Lemon 74

2 The Bottom Vegetable Drawer

APPLES, LEMONS 78

Potatoes, Lemon, Oregano 80

Chicken, Lemon, Tarragon 81

Avocado, Lemon, Coriander 84

Spinach, Lemon, Watercress 85

Apples For Duck Legs 86

Apfelküchlein 88

Ricotta, Lemon, Polenta Teacakes 92

Banana, Lemon Sorbet 94

Apple, Cinnamon, Oat Crumble 95

Beetroot, Dill, Apple 98

ROSEMARY, SAGE, THYME, BAY 102

Pork, Bay, Watercress 105

Swiss Chard, Rosemary, White Bean Soup 108

Veal, Bay, Carrots 114

Beans, Sage, Garlic 117

Salt Beef, Bay, Thyme 119

Venison, Bay, Prunes 122

Bean, Rosemary, Ham Hock Soup   123

Veal Chop, Sage, Lemon   124

3 The Fridge Door

EGGS, MILK   130

Chocolate Ice Cream   132

Fresh Mint Ice Cream   134

Gingerbread Ice Cream   138

Earl Grey Ice Cream   140

Josh's Morning Smoothie   141

Vanilla Custard   142

Rhubarb, Vanilla, Custard   144

Meringues 1   148

Meringues, Cream, Strawberries   150

Meringues 2   152

Aioli   153

CREAM, SOUR CREAM   154

Yoghurt   156

Aubergine, Lemon, Yoghurt   158

Carrot, Yoghurt, Cumin Soup   159

Yoghurt, Mint, Cucumbers   162

Yoghurt Ice Cream   164

Apricots, Vanilla, Yoghurt   165

Bircher Muesli   166

Muesli   168

Granola   172

Horseradish, Crème Fraîche, Lemon — 174

Leeks, Cream, Fennel — 175

Celeriac, Crème Fraîche, Mustard — 176

4 The Dry Stores Cupboard

NUTMEG, CINNAMON, GINGER — 180

Tomato, Cinnamon, Garlic — 182

Borlotti, Cinnamon, Tomato — 183

Green Beans, Cinnamon, Tomato — 184

Leek, Nutmeg, Cavolo Nero — 186

Celeriac, Nutmeg, Cream — 187

Chestnut, Nutmeg, Bacon Soup — 188

Pears, Cinnamon, Star Anise — 192

Carrot, Cinnamon, Walnut Cake — 194

Gingerbread — 200

Banana, Cinnamon, Pineapple Bread — 202

CORIANDER SEED, FENNEL SEED, CARAWAY SEED — 206

Josh's Virgin Mary — 208

Lamb, Coriander Seed, Garlic — 212

Aubergine, Coriander Seed, Currants — 213

Duck Leg, Fennel Seed, Cider — 214

Pork Cheek, Coriander Seed, Barley — 218

Lamb, Coriander Seed, Prunes — 222

Brussels Sprouts, Caraway Seed, Bacon — 225

Red Cabbage, Caraway Seed, Apple — 226

Potatoes, Fennel Seed, Garlic — 228

ANCHOVIES, DRIED MUSHROOMS, CAPERS, MUSTARD,
ROSE WATER, ORANGE FLOWER WATER, VINEGAR 230

Ox Cheek, Porcini, Tomato   234

Barley, Thyme, Porcini Soup   240

Celeriac, Anchovy, Mustard   242

Walnut Dressing, Salad Leaves   244

Onion Jam   245

Potatoes, Dill, Capers   246

Mr Abraham's Tomato Sauce   248

Lentils, Dill, Mustard   249

Salsa Verde   253

Pear, Lemon, Rose Sorbet   255

Carrots, Orange Blossom Water, Lemon   256

Blood Oranges, Mint, Rose Water   257

Index   261

Acknowledgements   269

Introduction

My fridge is my orchard: an urban orchard, at times lush and plentiful, at others, barren and sad. It is both the seasons and my disposition that dictate its offerings. On a freezing February day I return from the greengrocer empty-handed, tired of the winter vegetables and downhearted and I am scarcely able to fill its shelves. While with the warmth of a fine July afternoon I am cooking for two and feel hugely inspired. At least once a day, I find myself foraging in my fridge, harvesting its ingredients for a meal. This book is a selection of recipes from this harvest and a celebration of the feasts that result from the February and July days alike.

When I am cooking I feel steady and at home. I am often reminded of a time when I used to stand and cook next to my mother. The food we would prepare was the food I was built on: fruit, vegetables, herbs and meat in their simplest forms. Every day my mother would go to the market and buy as much fruit and as many vegetables as she could carry. She did not believe in an empty fridge – an empty fridge was an empty home, and her cooking was about generosity and abundance. Perhaps above all, cooking was for my mother about acknowledging and soothing a longing for her roots, locked under an Iron Curtain in Eastern Europe. For her and for my father, food was a way of bridging the gap between England and the countries they had left behind, a common language in which to narrate old memories and to create new ones. Whilst I have the good fortune of standing on home soil and speaking my mother tongue every day, my food and these recipes are rooted in Central and Eastern Europe.

On a Sunday night, after a weekend of treats, we would ask my mother what was for dinner. She'd promptly reply with a glint in her eye, 'fruits of the fridge, of course'. And we'd sit at the table and wait for a feast – lovingly crafted and skilfully re-invented. The remains of yesterday's potato salad would now be a

rösti, the pumpkin at the bottom of the fridge a fragrant soup using up the last of the chestnuts we'd roasted the night before. So our fridge became our orchard: a constantly evolving, plentiful and seasonal source of nourishment and creativity, and its fruits provided many a happy meal around our table. And in the same way, this book is also about feeding; the food in my fridge is nothing without my wooden spoon and my will to turn it into something for the table.

The way I see my fridge and my store cupboard informs the way I cook, and thus I have chosen to divide up the chapters in this book. There are three main sections to my fridge. Unless I have been away or unwell, there will always be eggs, milk and very often cream in my fridge door. My top vegetable drawer will almost always contain garlic, onions, parsley, dill, mint and, on good days, perhaps other fresh seasonal herbs. The bottom vegetable drawer holds the least perishable mainstays of my fridge. This is more often than not the most bountiful section, laden with hardy vegetables, such as potatoes, celeriac, carrots, Savoy cabbage and leeks; the more robust herbs – rosemary, thyme, sage and bay leaves; and staples such as apples and lemons. Finally there is the dry stores cupboard. This I try to keep quite well stocked with a few dried herbs and spices that I use frequently. These include fennel, caraway and coriander seeds, nutmeg, cinnamon, ginger, dried chilli, black peppercorns and plenty of Maldon sea salt. If I am able, I also rely on a stock of varying quantities of anchovies, dried wild mushrooms, mustard, capers and rose water. This cupboard is instrumental in 'emergency meals', those created in a limited amount of time based on a few available ingredients, as well as for seasoning braises and stews.

In between the fridge door and the two vegetable drawers lies uncertainty and special occasion. There may be some smoked bacon on the meat shelf. Perhaps some Stilton from last night's dinner party; a selection of fresh wild mushrooms from the farmers' market. However, these other 'guests' in the fridge are not fixtures. Such offerings are either the result of happy coincidence or conscious planning. A whole raw chicken does not ever happen to be lying around in my fridge, nor a venison haunch or a fresh goats' cheese. These are highly perishable and thus a luxury and a special treat.

And so I delight in opening the fridge door, having a mosey in the vegetable drawers, catching a whiff of an overly ripe cheese and deciding what feast I am going to create. In a culinary age where we are often entirely overwhelmed with choice, selecting just a few 'fruits of the fridge' with which to concoct a meal is the real adventure in cooking. And not only is it satisfying and rewarding, but this sort of cooking is undoubtedly economical.

I have come to enjoy the nature of my fridge, embracing the days of bare shelves and relishing those of plentiful abundance where merely a plate and a knife suffice for preparation. I hope to share this with you in these simple recipes. It is an orchard never quite without fruit; sometimes it just requires a little imagination.

Natalia

Cooking notes

Where possible, the ingredients specified in the book are as follows:

- Milk is full-fat (preferably organic)

- Parsley is flat-leaf

- Dried chillies are piquín or bird's eye

- Olive oil is extra virgin

- Butter is unsalted

- Salt is Maldon sea salt (NB don't waste this in boiling water, buy some coarse rock salt for seasoning boiling water)

- Ground black pepper is whole peppercorns pounded by hand in a pestle and mortar – this makes a difference!

A note on tools

You can pretty much cook on anything in anything, however, there are some guidelines that are best followed for longer cooking. Anything requiring time over a flame/hob should be cooked using the heaviest-bottomed pan that you have – this helps prevent the contents from burning but this is no guarantee. When making a soup, start with a pan that will be able to encompass the whole soup even if the initial 'base' ingredients don't seem like much; it's a pain to have to switch pans when you add the stock/water/cream. Also, all ovens vary so use the timings in this book as a rough guide – check the dish well before the end of the cooking time or leave in the oven for a few minutes more, if you need to. The latest mod cons are lovely but we cooked before and we'll cook after, so please don't ever feel that any of these recipes are out of your reach if you don't own them. An old wooden spoon and some energy is by and large my weapon of choice. Finally, whichever knife you use, it is a real treat to keep them sharp; cooking becomes so much more of a pleasure and apparently less dangerous!

A note on 'bases' and time

It might appear laborious that for many of my recipes you are required to cook
a 'base' – the name I use for variations on the theme of onions, garlic and celery
sweating in a saucepan of olive oil and/or butter – for up to an hour. I would
venture that you try to look at the timing in a positive way. One of my firm beliefs
in the kitchen is that the longer you leave the base to cook, the more delicious
your dish will be in the end. Allowing these vegetables to 'cook down' over a
long period of time enables you to get the most flavour and depth into them and
ultimately your dishes. Humble ingredients need time to impart their aromas.
If you can be patient you will reap the benefits. I also think there is a sort of
peacefulness about letting the ingredients do their thing. Once you get used to this
idea, I hope that you might like it.

Recipe titles

For the most part, I title my dishes according to the three main ingredients in the
recipe. The herb or spice is at the centre as they are such crucial elements. For
me herbs, spices and aromatics are very often the most valuable ingredient in a
dish and I try to keep them central to each. In Parsley, Peppers, Garlic (page 24),
for example, the parsley is where the dish begins – fried in abundance with garlic
and oil – and where it finishes, with fresh leaves chopped and sprinkled with a
heavy hand over the top of the serving dish at the table. With the Ricotta, Lemon,
Polenta Teacakes (page 92), the lemon juice and zest run through the cake, and
the final decoration is wafer-thin lemon segments. However, sometimes I've
veered from this where it really wouldn't make sense: meringues are meringues
after all – it would be a bit ridiculous to call them sugar, vanilla, egg!

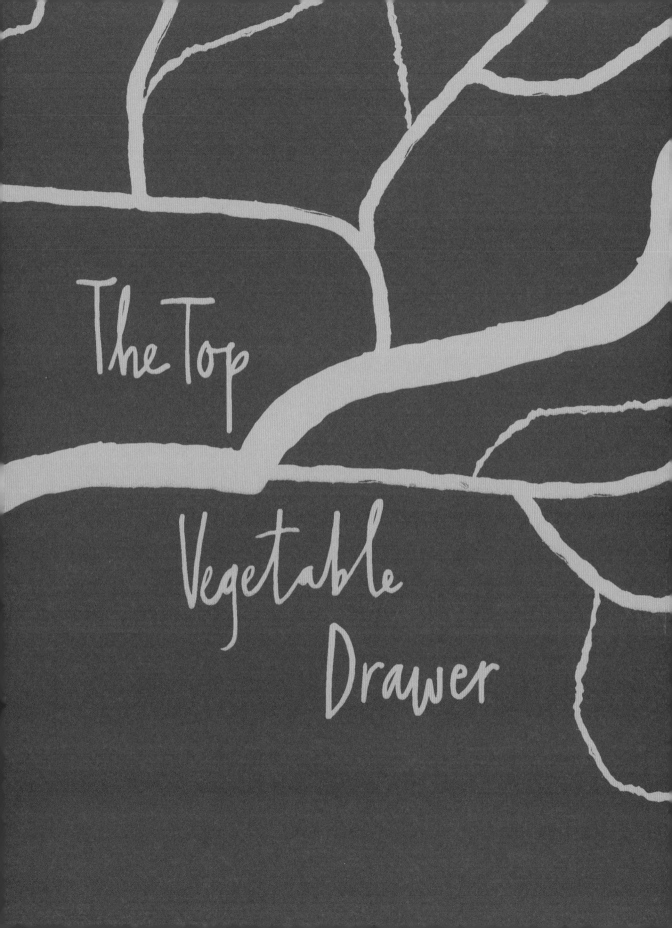

The Top Vegetable Drawer

Parsley, Garlic, Basil

Peppers, Parsley, Garlic 24

Carrots, Parsley, Honey 26

Chicken, Parsley, Green Beans 27

Swiss Chard, Parsley, Spinach 28

Chicken, Parsley, Carrot Soup 32

Fennel Broth, Parsley, Chicken 34

Lentils, Ramsons, Basil 36

Tomato, Parsley, Garlic 37

Chicken, Parsley, Breadcrumbs 38

Ham Hock, Parsley, Dandelion 41

Borlotti, Parsley, Bread Soup 47

Basil, Garlic, Pine Nuts 1 50

Basil, Garlic, Pine Nuts 2 51

Chickpeas, Garlic, Paprika 52

Peppers, parsley, garlic

I think that this dish is a great way of eating sweet red peppers when they are at their best at the height of summer. My mother used to make a version of this, which she called lecsó. It was her version of a Hungarian dish that her mother used to make, to which her mother added finely sliced onions, fresh dill and, at the end, a beaten egg stirred in and cooked by the heat of the dish.

SERVES 4 AS A SIDE DISH

- <u>8</u> sweet red peppers
- <u>2</u> tablespoons olive oil
- <u>4</u> garlic cloves, finely sliced
- <u>6</u> tablespoons flat-leaf parsley, roughly chopped, plus extra to finish
- • salt and freshly ground black pepper

Peel the peppers using a potato peeler. Peel them as if you were peeling an apple, working round the pepper but leave a gap between each circle. You should end up with a pepper that's half-peeled and looks stripey. Cut it in half and remove the seeds, then cut each half into medium strips (you should have stripes of skin along the length of each strip).

In a large heavy-bottomed saucepan, heat the olive oil over a medium heat. Add the garlic slices and leave to colour. Season generously with salt. When the garlic is golden brown and just starting to stick to the bottom of the pan and the wooden spoon, add the peppers and the parsley. Toss the contents of the pan about a bit, then reduce the heat and add 3 tablespoons of water. Cook covered, stirring regularly until the peppers are very soft – about 30 minutes. Finish with more chopped parsley and pepper.

Carrots, parsley, honey

These carrots make a great side dish for sausages or roast meat. I also like a large bowl of them on a cold night with a mustardy green salad and some warm bread.

SERVES 3 AS A SIDE DISH

6 tablespoons olive oil

10 carrots, washed thoroughly, roughly chopped into 1cm-thick diagonals

6 garlic cloves, peeled, finely sliced

1 tablespoon honey

4 tablespoons flat-leaf parsley leaves, roughly chopped

• salt and freshly ground black pepper

In a medium heavy-bottomed saucepan, gently heat the olive oil. Add the carrots to the pan and leave them to colour, adding a little salt. You want the carrots to really brown and almost catch at the bottom. Turn them and add the garlic slivers, allowing them to sizzle in the olive oil. Stir the carrots and garlic and add a couple of tablespoons of water to help loosen any bits of carrot that may have stuck to the bottom of the pan. Add the honey and continue to cook on a low heat. Finally, add the parsley, some freshly ground pepper and place a lid on the saucepan, leaving the carrots to cook on a very gentle heat. You want to cook the carrots until they are really starting to fall apart – about 30 minutes. During this time, if you feel that they are starting to burn at the bottom, add a splash more water.

Chicken, parsley, green beans

SERVES 4 AS A MAIN COURSE

300g boiled chicken (it would be good to use the boiled chicken from a chicken soup, see page 32)

10 tablespoons Basil, Garlic, Pine Nuts 1 (see page 50)

6 tablespoons whole parsley leaves

4 tablespoons coriander leaves

400g fine green beans, blanched until soft but still holding their shape

Toss the chicken with the basil sauce, herbs and the green beans until everything is mixed together well; it should be so well combined that each mouthful contains sauce, chicken, herbs and beans.

Swiss chard, parsley, spinach

The clean and fresh taste of this recipe serves as a lovely accompaniment to rich dishes.

SERVES 4 AS A SIDE DISH

4 tablespoons olive oil

3 garlic cloves, peeled and cut into fine slivers

1 bunch Swiss chard, leaves blanched, stalks roughly chopped into 1cm pieces and blanched until soft

500g spinach, blanched until soft in plenty of boiling salted water and drained well

- small handful capers

- juice of 2 lemons

1 bunch flat-leaf parsley leaves, finely chopped

- salt and freshly ground black pepper

In a medium saucepan, heat the olive oil and fry the garlic until golden brown. Add the Swiss chard leaves and stalks, spinach, capers and toss with the garlic and oil. Add the lemon juice and parsley. Check the seasoning and serve.

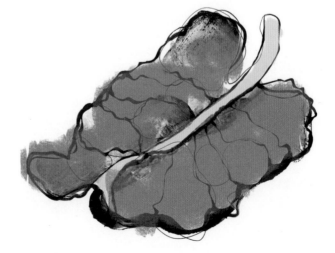

Chicken, parsley, carrot soup

The most stressful element of Jewish holidays for my mother was neither the gathering together of large numbers of Jewish friends and relatives, nor the possibly traumatic theme of the holiday, but rather more the ordeal of having to eat one of her friend's 'attempts' at chicken soup. 'Pond water' tended to be her description. A number of my recipes are variations on my mother's, however I do not believe this recipe can be bettered. So here it is in its most original form: chicken soup à la Katyushka, my mother.

NB If you are having this soup as a main course, you can also boil some pasta and mix it into the soup at the end. Stelline – 'little stars' – are ideal.

SERVES 6–8

1   large chicken, giblets removed

4   carrots, washed and halved

3   bay leaves

6   peppercorns

2   red onions, skin on, halved

2   parsnips, halved

3   leeks, roughly chopped

½   Savoy cabbage, quartered

1   tomato

2   heads garlic, skin on, sliced horizontally through the middle

3   large handfuls flat-leaf parsley, stalks intact, plus a large handful of finely chopped leaves for the garnish

Place all of the ingredients in a very large pot with enough cold water to cover the bird by 2.5cm. Bring to the boil and simmer for as long as possible, ideally for 3–4 hours, with the lid on, though slightly ajar. Depending on how much fat you enjoy in your chicken soup (I like the flavour it gives), take a ladle and carefully skim off about half. You can of course remove all the fat should you so desire.

Remove the chicken and discard the skin and cartilage, carefully removing any small bones as well. Take the meat off the carcass and tear the meat into pieces. I like mine just roughly broken with a fork so that you can identify breast and leg meat.

Pour the soup through a sieve then divide between bowls. Add the chicken and sprinkle generously with the chopped parsley. Finally, fish the 'soupy' carrots, leeks and cabbage out of the pot and add them to the bowls. Enjoy.

Fennel broth, parsley, chicken

SERVES 6–8

6	tablespoons olive oil
10	fennel bulbs, trimmed and cut into quarters
6	garlic cloves, finely sliced
1	tablespoon ground fennel seeds
2 litres	hot Chicken, Parsley, Carrot Soup (see page 32)
•	salt, to taste
•	roughly chopped parsley, to serve

In a wide heavy-bottomed saucepan, heat the olive oil over a medium heat. When the oil is hot, brown the fennel on all sides. It is good to add the salt at this point. Add the garlic slices and allow a few minutes for the garlic to become golden. Add 150ml water, the ground fennel seeds, stir well and reduce the heat. Place a lid on the pot and cook for a further 35–40 minutes or until the fennel is extremely soft and mushy, a bit like apple compote in appearance; there should be no bite to it whatsoever. Finally stir the fennel in to the hot chicken stock. Serve topped with plenty of chopped parsley.

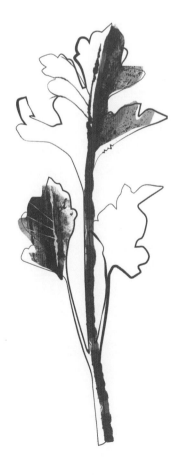

Lentils, ramsons, basil

This thick and warming soup is a lovely way to show off the fragrant flavour of ramsons (wild garlic) when it is in season, usually late February to May here in the UK.

SERVES 8 AS A MAIN COURSE

6 tablespoons olive oil, plus some extra for serving

5 garlic cloves, finely chopped

3 red onions, roughly diced

1 celery head, roughly diced

2 leeks, green parts removed, roughly diced

4 tablespoons whole basil leaves

3 carrots, peeled and roughly diced

3 parsnips, peeled and roughly diced

500g dried lentils (Puy or Castelluccio are best), boiled in plenty of water with half a head of garlic until extremely soft – about 1 hour

4 large slices ciabatta or a similar white bread with little salt, crusts removed

3 tablespoons roughly chopped ramsons (if you can't find ramsons, the green tops of spring onions will do fine)

• salt and freshly ground black pepper

In a large, heavy-bottomed pot, heat the oil over a medium heat and fry the garlic and onions together with some salt for about 10 minutes. Add the celery, leeks, half the basil leaves, carrots and parsnips and cook for about 50 minutes, stirring the pot with a wooden spoon from time to time. When the vegetables are extremely soft, add the cooked lentils, some more salt and pepper and the remaining basil leaves. Stir well.

Place the slices of bread over the soup to form a sort of lid. Pour enough boiling water over the bread to cover and place a lid on the pot. Continue to cook over a very low heat for a further 5–10 minutes. Remove the lid, add the ramsons and gently fold the soft bread into the rest of the soup. Add more boiling water if the soup is too thick; it should be a thick soup but still liquid enough to eat easily with a spoon rather than a knife and fork! Check for seasoning and serve with plenty more olive oil and pepper.

Tomato, parsley, garlic

The parsley in this sauce can be exchanged for basil, oregano or marjoram, or anything you fancy. You can also add olives or anchovies or pancetta. It can form the base of your Bolognese or baked eggs in tomato. Basically it's just guidance for the tomato sauce I like to make. The sauce goes nicely with pasta as well as on top of boiled lentils or chickpeas.

SERVES 6 AS A SAUCE FOR PASTA

3 tablespoons olive oil, plus some extra-virgin olive oil to finish

6 garlic cloves, finely sliced

5 tablespoons flat-leaf parsley, finely chopped

1kg plum tomatoes, peeled, roughly chopped

• salt and freshly ground black pepper

In a heavy-bottomed saucepan, heat the olive oil over a medium heat and add the garlic slices. Season generously with salt. When the garlic starts to turn golden, it will start to stick to the bottom of the pan and the wooden spoon. At this point, and before it is too brown, add the parsley and fry. The parsley will pop and spatter a bit, so watch out. Fry for about 30 seconds then add the chopped tomato. Add some more salt (tomatoes, like potatoes, need plenty of salt), pepper and leave to simmer for about an hour. When the sauce is ready, it will be deeper in colour and will have come together, be unctuous and without excess water. Finish with a drizzle of the best extra-virgin olive oil you can find.

Chicken, parsley, breadcrumbs

In Austria a Wiener schnitzel is traditionally made with veal or pork (Wiener schnitzel vom schwein), however chicken was the meat my mother used in our schnitzels at home, so that is what I have chosen for the recipe below. While each meat has a delicious result it is perhaps worth considering that veal is the significantly more costly option.

SERVES 4 AS A MAIN COURSE

300g homemade fresh breadcrumbs (place a roughly torn loaf of crustless bread into a food processor and pulse until you have a rough crumb)

1 egg, beaten with 250ml whole milk

250g plain flour, seasoned generously with salt and pepper

4 chicken breasts, beaten to about 1cm thickness (you can ask your butcher to do this or simply place the breasts in a plastic freezer bag and beat gently with a rolling pin)

at least 1.5 litres sunflower oil

1 bunch flat-leaf parsley, leaves only

• salt and freshly ground black pepper

• lemon wedges, to serve

Put the breadcrumbs, egg mixture and flour into three separate bowls. Take each chicken breast and dip it first into the egg mixture, then in the seasoned flour, then back into the egg mixture and finally into the breadcrumbs.

Fill the largest pot you have with sunflower oil so that the level of oil reaches a third of the way up the sides. Heat the oil until extremely hot – drop a couple of breadcrumbs in and see if they fizz vigorously in the oil; this will mean that the oil is hot enough. Drop the crumbed chicken into the hot oil two breasts at a time. Try not to move the chicken around too much. When the underside is golden brown turn the chicken breast and allow the other side to brown. When both sides are nicely golden, remove the breasts and allow them to dry on plenty of kitchen paper, while you repeat the process with the other two. Sprinkle generously with salt and pepper while still hot.

Continues overleaf

Continued from page 38

When all of the chicken has been cooked, turn off the heat. Take the parsley and drop it into the oil. Retire a good distance immediately as the parsley will spit for a few moments before becoming crispy. Remove the parsley with a slotted spoon and drain on kitchen paper. Serve the chicken with the fried parsley and lemon wedges.

I like to serve this with the Potatoes, Dill, Capers (see page 246). And although it might raise eye brows, I think no schnitzel is complete without a large dollop of tomato ketchup!

If you have any leftover schnitzel, try it sliced in a ciabatta-bread sandwich along with some Celeriac, Crème fraîche, Mustard (page 176).

Ham hock, parsley, dandelion

SERVES 6 AS A MAIN COURSE SALAD

1   raw, medium-sized ham hock, brined and ready to cook (this is a fairly inexpensive cut that can be ordered from most butchers)

2   celery sticks

1   red onion, skin on, halved

3   bay leaves

1   head garlic, skin on, halved, plus 2 garlic cloves, peeled and crushed

1   bunch parsley, stalks and leaves separated

100ml   golden syrup

•   small handful fennel seeds, pounded in a pestle and mortar

100ml   olive oil, plus a little extra to dress the salad

•   large handful whole cloves

3   bunches yellow dandelions, roughly chopped

2   bunches watercress, roughly chopped

2   tablespoons Dijon mustard

1   tablespoon sherry vinegar

2   tablespoons capers

•   salt and freshly ground black pepper

Place the ham hock, celery, onion, bay leaves, head of garlic and parsley stalks in a large pot with enough water to cover the hock. Bring to the boil and simmer gently for 2¼ hours, until the meat is very tender. While the meat is cooking, put the golden syrup in a saucepan and add the fennel seeds, crushed garlic cloves and olive oil. Heat gently until the ingredients are combined.

Preheat the oven to 225°C/Gas 7½. When cooked, remove the hock and place on a roasting tray. Make diagonal cuts in the fat surrounding the hock and spike with cloves. Pour over the golden syrup mixture, rubbing it into all the nooks and crannies of the hock. Remember not to add salt to the hock as it is already brined, however do add some freshly ground pepper. Place the hock in the oven and roast until the skin is a dark molasses brown and blisteringly crisp – it takes about 20 minutes, then remove from the oven and leave until cool enough to handle.

Continues overleaf

Continued from page 41

Place the dandelion and watercress in a large
mixing bowl with the whole parsley leaves.
Season with salt, pepper and a little olive oil.
When the hock is cold enough to handle,
pull the meat from the bone, chop the skin,
discarding any large lumps of fat that have not
crisped up, and dress with the mustard, sherry
vinegar, capers, some of the roasting juices and
black pepper. Gently combine the two mixtures
and serve.

At least once a day I find myself foraging in my fridge, harvesting its ingrediants for a meal.

Borlotti, parsley, bread soup

Every year in November a few chefs from The River Café head out to Tuscany to taste and bring home the new season's olive oil. One year I was lucky enough to be part of the trip. With wine and olive oil tastings from 9 o'clock in the morning and the most beautiful meals hosted within the old stone walls of the Felsina, Selvapiana, Capezzana and Fontodi estates, it was truly a culinary trip that will stay with me for life. It was fascinating to observe the differences between the estates and meet the families whose characters shape and flavour everything from the appearance of their vineyards and wine cellars, to the intensity of their olive oil and the nose on their wines. More than anything, I began to realise just how extraordinary the olive oils that we were using in the restaurant were. It was an unexpected realisation and it gave me the highest regard for the magnificent oil with which we were so liberally allowed and encouraged to season almost all of our dishes. Watching the process and seeing just how much effort and how many olives (of which there were very few that year) it took to make a bottle of olive oil, I found that on my return to the kitchen, I poured the olive oil over my dishes with no less gusto but with a new sense of excitement and reverence.

Hosted by Giovanni Manetti at his Fontodi estate in Panzano, we were offered a fantastic soup on the top of which he showcased a full inch of his luminescent green, hour-old olive oil. So thick was the soup that you could eat it with a knife and fork, its earthy hues telling of slow cooking and concentration of flavours. It was fantastic and I subsequently devoured two whole bowls. I tried to recreate this soup – a ribollita – back in London and this is my recipe.

Borlotti, parsley, bread soup

SERVES 6–8 AS A MAIN COURSE

6 tablespoons olive oil

3 red onions, finely chopped

5 garlic cloves, finely chopped

3 carrots, roughly chopped

2 heads celery, outer branches removed, hearts roughly chopped

1 bunch parsley leaves, roughly chopped

5 tablespoons tinned chopped tomatoes

1 bunch cavolo nero (or the outer leaves)

500g cooked borlotti beans (see page 117), cooking liquor reserved

¾ loaf stale white bread (ciabatta is fine too), crust removed, cut into 2.5cm thick wedges

• plenty of the best olive oil you can find

600ml boiling water

• salt and freshly ground black pepper

In a large heavy-bottomed pot, fry the onions, garlic, carrots, celery and parsley in the olive oil for about 1 hour over a low heat (don't cover the pot).

When these are entirely soft, add the tomato and continue to cook down for a further 15 minutes. Stir in the cavolo nero and set aside.

Pour half of the beans with half their cooking liquid into a food processor. Pulse until smooth then add to the vegetables. Strain the other half of the beans and add them to the soup. Finally place the bread gently on top of the soup to form a sort of lid. Cover with plenty of olive oil. Pour the boiling water over the bread then allow the soup to cook very gently for 10 minutes then to sit for a further 10 minutes. The bread should be completely soft. Gently break up the bread lid and fold it in to the rest of the soup. Check for seasoning and serve with some more olive oil on top – the soup should be thick enough so that you can stand up a spoon in it.

Basil, garlic, pine nuts 1

This is a kind of 'lighter' pesto made without the Parmesan cheese. I like to spoon this over boiled asparagus, poached chicken in a sandwich or even – rather indulgently – over fresh mozzarella. For a pesto that's better suited to being spooned over pasta or gnocchi, see the next recipe.

SERVES 10–12 AS A SAUCE FOR BOILED VEGETABLES OR MEAT

150g pine nuts

1 garlic clove, mashed to a paste with the back of a knife and some salt

• very large bunch basil, leaves only

275ml best olive oil

75ml milk

• salt and freshly ground black pepper

In a food processor, pulse the pine nuts and garlic with some salt and pepper – watch the salt, a little goes a long way in this sauce. Add the basil and pour in the olive oil, continuing to pulse. Finally add the milk, blending until you have a very smooth, vibrant green sauce. Allow the sauce to sit for a few minutes before checking for seasoning.

Basil, garlic, pine nuts 2

This pesto recipe should be considerably thicker than the previous one and is best suited as a sauce for gnocchi or pasta.

SERVES 4 ON PASTA (APPROXIMATELY 10 TABLESPOONS)

1 garlic clove, peeled

200ml olive oil

2 tablespoons pine nuts

½ bunch basil leaves

3 tablespoons grated Parmesan

• salt and freshly ground black pepper

In a food processor, pulse the garlic, 50ml of the olive oil and some salt and pepper for about a minute – watch the salt though, a little goes a long way in this recipe as the Parmesan adds to the saltiness as well. Add the pine nuts and basil and pulse for a further 30 seconds. Add the Parmesan and remaining olive oil. Pulse for a minute. Check the consistency; you're aiming for quite a thick, spoonable paste, but if it is too thick add some more olive oil. Check the seasoning.

Chickpeas, garlic, paprika

This chickpea purée is quick and simple to make and is a very useful provision to have tucked away in the fridge. It's similar to hummus but doesn't include any tahini and the garlic is cooked rather than raw. Slightly warmed it's a gentle but filling accompaniment for meat and fish main courses. It also works well as a cold dip for bread or raw vegetables too.

SERVES 6-8 AS A SIDE DISH

<u>500g</u> dried chickpeas, soaked in plenty of water for at least 12 hours

<u>2</u> heads garlic, skin on, sliced horizontally through the middle

<u>6–8</u> tablespoons olive oil

<u>1</u> tablespoon sweet smoked paprika

• salt and freshly ground black pepper

Put the chickpeas and both heads of garlic into a large saucepan with plenty of water, enough to cover the chickpeas with another couple of centimetres above them.

Boil for anywhere between $1\frac{1}{2}$ hours and $2\frac{3}{4}$ hours – the time seems to depend so much on the chickpeas. Keep boiling until the chickpeas are really soft. Try one. If they are not completely tender, this dish will not work. Have faith and keep boiling.

When the chickpeas are about 5 minutes from being ready, add salt and pepper. Boil for a further 5 minutes then turn off the heat. Allow the chickpeas to sit and absorb any remaining seasoning. Remove the garlic heads from the liquid, scrape the tender garlic cloves from the whole bulbs and discard any tough bits of garlic skin.

In a food processor, blend half the chickpeas and all of the garlic cloves with enough of the chickpea water to help loosen the purée. Start with about 3 tablespoons. You need just enough to start to turn the purée ever so slightly paler in colour. Go gently with it though as it is very easy to end up with soup, and you've still the oil to add.

Spoon the purée into a bowl, add the olive oil – as much as you wish, and keep tasting. Stir in the drained whole chickpeas and check the seasoning. Finally, sprinkle the sweet smoked paprika on top.

NB If you are going to keep the purée in the fridge, it should keep for about 2–3 days. It keeps better if you store it in an airtight container with a layer of olive oil on top and a piece of baking paper under the lid.

Dill, Mint

Aubergines, Mint, Raisins 56

Aubergines, Dill, Potatoes 58

Khobez, Mint, Lemon 59

Tomatoes, Dill, Sherry Vinegar 60

Kohlrabi, Mint, Smoked Paprika 62

Peas, Mint, Dill 63

Peas, Dill, Little Gem Lettuce 64

Courgettes, Mint, Ricotta 66

Honey, Dill, Mustard 69

Green Leaves, Dill, Radish 70

Lamb Chops, Mint, Lemon 74

Aubergines, mint, raisins

This recipe is based on the Sicilian aubergine dish, caponata. There are many variations, some recipes include olives, carrots and even potatoes. I first learned to cook this at home with my mother. I particularly enjoy this with some grilled lamb or pork.

SERVES 4 AS A SIDE DISH

2 tablespoons pine nuts

• at least 1 litre sunflower oil

1 aubergine (about 400g), cut into 2cm cubes

3 tablespoons red wine vinegar

2 tablespoons olive oil

1 onion, finely diced

2 garlic cloves, finely diced

1½ tablespoons honey

4 large plum tomatoes, blanched in boiling water, then peeled, seeded and roughly diced

200g celery, roughly chopped and boiled until soft

2 tablespoons fresh finely chopped mint leaves

1 tablespoon capers

1 tablespoon raisins

• salt

Gently toast the pine nuts on a baking sheet in a low oven (about 150°C/Gas 2) until golden.

Boil some water and pour it over the tomatoes – the skin will start to peel away. After about 30 seconds in the hot water, put the tomatoes into another bowl with ice and water.

Fill the largest pot you have with sunflower oil so that the level of oil reaches one third of the way up the sides. Heat the oil until extremely hot – drop a cube of aubergine in: if it fizzes vigorously, the oil is hot enough. Fry the aubergine in batches and when dark golden on all sides, drain on plenty of kitchen paper. While the aubergines are still hot, sprinkle with 1 tablespoon of the vinegar and some salt.

In a saucepan, heat the olive oil over a medium heat and fry the onions and garlic with the honey. Season with salt and pepper and when they are very soft – about 15 minutes – add the tomato and celery.

Finally, in a large mixing bowl, toss the aubergine with the tomato mixture, remaining vinegar, mint, capers, raisins and pine nuts. Check the seasoning and serve.

Aubergines, dill, potatoes

This dish finds inspiration in cianfotta, a Neapolitan summer vegetable stew, something not dissimilar to a French ratatouille. In this recipe I have chosen to add dill. I've also kept the new potatoes whole with their skins on because I like having their distinct, imperfect shapes identifiable within the stew.

SERVES 4 AS A SIDE DISH

400g	new potatoes (Ratte potatoes are brilliant if you can get them)
4	tablespoons olive oil
2	onions, finely sliced
1	large red pepper, finely sliced
2	garlic cloves, finely sliced
4	tablespoons chopped dill
600g	tinned chopped tomatoes
•	at least 1.5 litres sunflower oil
1	aubergine (about 400g), cut into 2cm cubes

Place the potatoes in a saucepan of cold, salted water, bring to the boil and cook until soft – about 25 minutes.

In another saucepan, heat the olive oil over a low heat and fry the onion, pepper, garlic and two thirds of the dill until very soft – about 20 minutes, stirring from time to time. Add the tomatoes and cook for a further 30 minutes or until you have a very thick sauce.

Finally, fill the largest pot you have with sunflower oil so that the level of oil reaches a third of the way up the sides. Heat the oil until extremely hot – drop a cube of aubergine in: if it fizzes vigorously, the oil is hot enough. Fry the aubergine in batches and when dark golden on all sides, drain on plenty of kitchen paper. Toss the aubergines with the tomato sauce and potatoes and top with the remaining dill.

Khobez, mint, lemon

These Lebanese bread 'crisps' are a great baked alternative to fried potato chips. Khobez is a Lebanese flat bread that is widely available in Middle Eastern supermarkets. If you can't find khobez, pitta breads will do just fine. Serve these with something like hummus or Yoghurt, Mint, Cucumbers (see page 162).

SERVES 4–6 AS A SNACK OR WITH DRINKS

200g	khobez or pitta bread, sliced into 2cm strips
1	tablespoon dried mint
1	teaspoon dried oregano
3	tablespoons best olive oil
•	zest of ½ lemon
•	salt

Preheat the oven to 180°C/Gas 4.

Place the khobez on a baking tray. Sprinkle with the mint, oregano and salt, and drizzle with 2 tablespoons of the olive oil. Bake the bread for about 10 minutes, until crisp. Remove from the oven and toss with the remaining olive oil and lemon zest. These are best served warm but are good cold too.

Tomatoes, dill, sherry vinegar

SERVES 4 AS A SIDE DISH

12 very ripe medium tomatoes, (plum or ox heart are good), eye removed and a small cross cut just into the skin of each

4 shallots, peeled and very finely sliced

4 tablespoons sherry vinegar

2 teaspoons caster sugar

4 tablespoons olive oil

3 tablespoons chopped dill

• salt and freshly ground black pepper

Boil some water and pour it over the tomatoes – the skin will start to peel away. After about 30 seconds in the hot water, put the tomatoes into another bowl with ice and water.

In a separate bowl, mix the shallots with the vinegar, sugar and olive oil. Add salt and pepper. Peel the tomatoes and finely slice them. Put them on a plate and cover them with the dressed shallots and the dill.

Kohlrabi, mint, smoked paprika

This is a lovely fresh pickled salad that is particularly good with cold meats or smoked fish.

SERVES 6 AS A SIDE DISH

3   kohlrabi, peeled and finely sliced by hand, on a mandoline or in a food processor

2   tablespoons sweet smoked paprika

5   tablespoons white wine vinegar

2   tablespoons caster sugar

1   pinch dried chilli

1   tablespoon extra-virgin olive oil

4   tablespoons finely chopped mint, plus 2 tablespoons whole mint leaves to serve

•   salt and freshly ground black pepper

Mix the ingredients with the chopped mint, in a bowl. Check for seasoning. There should be a nice balance between sweet and sour; if this is not clear enough, adding a little more salt can help. Cover and leave in the fridge overnight to marinate. Serve with the additional whole mint leaves stirred through.

Peas, mint, dill

The result of cooking these peas very slowly is that they are sweet and somewhere between mushy and tinned pea consistency. These are a great accompaniment to meat and fish dishes; perhaps try them with the lamb chops on page 74 and the Yoghurt, Mint, Cucumbers on page 162.

SERVES 2 AS A SIDE DISH

30g   butter

3   garlic cloves, finely sliced

3   tablespoons mint leaves

2   tablespoons roughly chopped dill

300g   fresh peas, shelled

•   salt and freshly ground black pepper

In a heavy-bottomed saucepan, heat the butter over a medium heat and fry the garlic with some salt until the garlic begins to turn a pale golden colour. Add the mint and the dill and fry for a minute or so. Pour in the peas and stir with a wooden spoon. Sprinkle with a little more salt and some pepper. Add 200ml of water and place a cartouche (see page 105) over the top. Cover the saucepan with a tight-fitting lid and cook the peas on a low heat for 40 minutes, stirring occasionally, until the peas are entirely soft and a bit mushy.

Peas, dill, little gem lettuce

SERVES 4 AS A SIDE DISH

550g	fresh peas, shelled
4	Little Gem lettuces
1	garlic clove, peeled and finely sliced
2	tablespoons olive oil
1	bunch dill leaves, finely chopped
100ml	double cream
•	salt

Boil the peas in a saucepan of boiling water until tender. Depending on the time of year and size/freshness of the peas, they take anything from 3–20 minutes to be cooked. You just want to avoid a hard mealy pea. I'm not fussed about the vibrancy of the pea – if it needs to be more yellowy brown to be cooked properly that's fine with me.

Slice the bottom off the lettuces and peel apart the leaves.

In a pan, fry the garlic slices in the olive oil and plenty of salt until slightly coloured. Add the lettuce and reduce the heat. Add a splash of water and place the lid on for a few minutes so as to wilt the lettuce. When the leaves are soft, add the peas and dill and finally the cream. Leave on the heat for a brief moment or so to gently warm the peas and cream – be careful as you don't want to cook the cream.

Courgettes, mint, ricotta

At The River Café, where I learned this dish, they serve it topped with slowly cooked onions, Swiss chard leaves and ricotta. I often use the pastry recipe at home, as a sort of pizza/flat tart base and top it with whatever I can lay my hands on: sometimes tomato sauce (see page 37), with ricotta and anchovies or salami, or sometimes I leave it white, without sauce, and layer it with different cheeses and some fried courgettes. It's great informal party food if you're standing up. I like to put it in the middle of the table next to a bowl of salad and have a slice with a beer. If you're going to go for the first topping option (opposite), I'd really urge you to try and hunt down some robiola cheese rather than trying to substitute it. Being a mixture of three milks – goat, cow and sheep – it's got such a unique flavour that for me it really helps set this dish apart as something special.

SERVES 4–6

For the pastry:

225g   cold butter, cut into cubes

360g   plain flour

1   teaspoon salt

6   tablespoons iced water

Preheat the oven to 200°C/Gas 6.

Place the butter, flour and salt in a food processor and pulse until you have a very coarse crumb. Add the water and continue to pulse until the pastry is just holding together. Tip the mixture out on to a clean surface and bring it together gently with your hands into a log shape. Wrap it in cling film and chill for at least an hour.

Using the larger holes of a cheese grater, grate the pastry on to a baking tray (roughly 30 x 25cm). Lightly press down the pastry – you want to touch it as little as possible; it is good if you can see the rough outlines of the grated pieces of pastry.

Suggestions for the toppings:

1.

<u>400ml</u> sunflower oil

<u>150g</u> courgette (about <u>2</u> medium/small
courgettes – the smaller you can find
the better: small courgettes
create the best disc shapes and tend to
be less watery, which is key for this dish)

• salt

<u>10</u> whole fresh mint

<u>1</u> tablespoon red wine vinegar

<u>350g</u> ricotta mixed with <u>2</u> egg yolks and
<u>250g</u> grated Parmesan

<u>6</u> tablespoons chopped rocket, to serve

<u>150g</u> robiola cheese

<u>100g</u> mozzarella (buffalo mozzarella is nice
here too)

2.

<u>8</u> tablespoons tomato and basil sauce
(see page 37)

<u>250g</u> ricotta mixed with 2 egg yolks and
<u>150g</u> grated Parmesan

<u>200g</u> sliced salami

<u>3</u> tablespoons oregano leaves

If you are making topping 1: In a saucepan deep enough to contain 2.5 litres of liquid, heat the sunflower oil. Meanwhile, slice the courgettes into round discs, as thin as you can manage, working your way from one end of the courgette to the other. Place the rounds on absorbent kitchen towel and leave to dry for a few minutes (if time allows, do this before you heat the oil, and leave to dry for up to an hour). Test the temperature of the oil by dipping one courgette disc into it. It should fizz and pop vigorously. Fry the courgettes in batches; it is important not to overload the saucepan to ensure that the temperature of the oil stays as hot as possible. With a slotted spoon or tongs, turn the courgettes regularly so that they get a nice golden brown on all sides. When the courgettes are ready they will be crisp (depending on the size of the courgettes, this should take about 5 minutes). Remove from the pan and place immediately on plenty of absorbent kitchen towel. Sprinkle with salt whilst they are still hot. Finally, in a mixing bowl, toss the courgettes with the mint leaves and the vinegar. Check for seasoning.

For either topping: Bake the pastry for about 10 minutes, until just lightly golden. Add your selected toppings in even layers, season with some salt, pepper and olive oil, then bake for a further 20 minutes or so until the cheese is golden and has melted in to the vegetables and the pastry is golden brown on the edges.

Honey, dill, mustard

I eat this dressing in a salad of chopped green leaves: maybe Little Gem lettuce and a round lettuce together with some dill. If you're feeling up to it, layer a few rashers of bacon and some baked ricotta or Greek manouri cheese on top.

SERVES 6–8 AS A DRESSING FOR A SIDE SALAD

¼ garlic clove, mashed to a paste with some salt

2 tablespoons honey, dissolved in a few spoonfuls of boiling water

1 tablespoon mustard

2 tablespoons finely chopped dill

200ml best olive oil

1 tablespoon red wine vinegar

• salt and freshly ground black pepper

Mix the garlic, honey, mustard and dill together. Add the olive oil and finally the vinegar, whisking furiously with a fork. Add salt and pepper and allow the mixture to sit for a few minutes before having a further taste to check the seasoning.

Green leaves, dill, radish

This is a good, mostly green-leaf salad. I have decided to list ingredients without quantities here as I think that it should be up to the cook where they wish the balance of herbs and leaves to lie. I always have a heavy hand with fresh soft herbs. On the other hand, I have detailed the method of preparing each component; I think that the way in which salad leaves are prepared and cut is almost the most important. A green salad for me has to be beautiful to look at – almost popping out from the plate, like a picture out of a gardening book. Sian, my ex-head chef, always used to say this.

I think a soft leaf salad must ideally be prepared at the last minute and dressed at the table to avoid it becoming limp. It is a very different sort of animal to a chopped salad or any of my 'remoulade' style salads: shredded root vegetables with a heavy, strong dressing, which benefit from lengthy 'steeping' or marinating overnight.

radishes, buy only those in bright red bunches, which are very firm to the touch and with plenty of green leaves

Little Gem lettuce, sliced in half lengthways, then sliced again lengthways into thirds

large dark green watercress, roughly torn into sprigs

mint leaves

roughly chopped dill

finely chopped chives

lemon

best olive oil

- salt and freshly ground black pepper

Discard the leaves and stalks of the radishes, then slice them into fine slivers or quarters – both are nice. Place your leaves, herbs and radishes in a large bowl and gently season with salt and pepper. Squeeze over some lemon juice and toss the leaves delicately with your fingers, adding generous amounts of your best olive oil as you turn the leaves gently over in the bowl. Serve immediately.

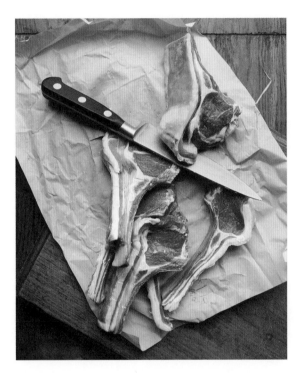

Lamb chops, mint, lemon

I like to serve these chops with an aubergine salad or the Yoghurt, Mint, Cucumbers on page 162 and my khobez bread crisps (see page 59).

SERVES 2 AS A MAIN COURSE

about 6 lamb chops (rib chops with plenty of fat and meat on the bone are best, not 'French-trimmed')

4 tablespoons extra-virgin olive oil

1 lemon, halved, plus extra wedges

1 tablespoon dried peppermint

1 teaspoon dried oregano

• best olive oil

• salt and freshly ground black pepper

Remove the lamb from the fridge about 1 hour before cooking. Pat the chops dry with kitchen paper and season generously with salt.

Heat a frying pan until it looks like it is starting to smoke then immediately add the oil then the lamb chops. Don't add the oil before the pan is hot – if you heat the oil you may end up burning it. Brown the lamb chops until golden on both sides – about $1\frac{1}{2}$ minutes on each side. I like my lamb very pink but it's up to your taste – cook them a little longer if you like them slightly more done. To check for doneness make an incision with a knife. Remove the chops from the heat and squeeze the lemon over the meat, then sprinkle over the mint and oregano and some black pepper. Rest the chops in the pan for about 3 minutes and serve with some more lemon squeezed over and a large glug of your best olive oil. Eat these hot or room temperature in warmer weather, and with your fingers.

The
Bottom Vegetable
Drawer

Apples, Lemons

Potatoes, Lemon, Oregano 80

Chicken, Lemon, Tarragon 81

Avocado, Lemon, Coriander 84

Spinach, Lemon, Watercress 85

Apples For Duck Legs 86

Apfelküchlein 88

Ricotta, Lemon, Polenta Teacakes 92

Banana, Lemon Sorbet 94

Apple, Cinnamon, Oat Crumble 95

Beetroot, Dill, Apple 98

Potatoes, lemon, oregano

SERVES 4 AS A SIDE DISH

800g waxy new potatoes (Roseval or Pink Fir Apple are good)

6 tablespoons olive oil

25g butter

½ tablespoon dried oregano

½ tablespoon dried mint

• juice of 1 lemon

• salt and freshly ground black pepper

Boil the new potatoes, skin on, in plenty of salted water, until tender but not crumbling – about 15 minutes, although it can take up to 30 depending on your potatoes, so just keep checking until you're happy they're ready. With a sharp knife, slice the potatoes in half lengthways.

In a frying pan, heat the olive oil over a medium heat. Place the potatoes in the oil, skin-side up, and leave to colour. You want a nice golden brown so that they are crispy. Turn the potatoes the other side up and add the butter, oregano, mint and lemon juice. Toss the potatoes about in the butter and quickly take them off the heat (you don't want the butter to burn!). Check the seasoning and serve immediately.

Chicken, lemon, tarragon

This is my recipe for roast chicken. It is a pot roast and so it is very simply made. You can serve it with roast potatoes, chips, rice, soft polenta or it is lovely with the Celeriac, Nutmeg, Cream on page 187 and the Green Leaves, Dill, Radish on page 70.

SERVES 4 (OR 2 WITH SOME LEFT OVER FOR SANDWICHES IN THE MORNING!)

1	medium chicken
1	lemon, quartered
125g	butter
1	bunch thyme or tarragon
1	red onion, skin on, quartered
2	heads garlic, skin on, sliced horizontally through the middle
750ml	white wine or half water, half wine
3	bay leaves
•	salt and freshly ground black pepper

Preheat the oven to 180°C/Gas 4.

Put all of the ingredients with plenty of salt and pepper in a pot with a tight-fitting lid. In the event that you don't have a pot with a fitting lid, use a roasting tin wrapped tightly with several layers of aluminium foil. Make sure the liquid comes halfway up the sides of the bird.

Place the pot in the oven and cook for about 1½ hours, or until the legs can easily be pulled away from the main cavity and the meat is very soft. Turn the oven up to its maximum. Remove the lid and cook uncovered for a further 15–20 minutes, until the skin is crisp and golden.

Our fridge became our orchard: a constantly evolving, plentiful and seasonal source of nourishment and creativity.

Avocado, lemon, coriander

SERVES 4–6 AS A GENEROUS SIDE DISH OR ON TOAST

4 large, very ripe avocados, peeled and stoned (about 700g in weight without stones or skin)

50ml olive oil

• juice of 1 lemon

2 tablespoons roughly chopped coriander

• salt and freshly ground black pepper

Place the avocado in a bowl. With a fork, gently break up the avocado and mix in the olive oil, lemon and coriander until you have a chunky, uneven mixture. Season generously with salt and pepper, allowing the mixture to sit for a few minutes before tasting and re-seasoning.

Spinach, lemon, watercress

SERVES 2 AS A SIDE DISH

500g   spinach

1½   tablespoons lemon juice

3   tablespoons chopped watercress (leaves and stalks)

4   tablespoons olive oil

2   tablespoons chopped dill

•   salt and freshly ground black pepper

Boil the baby spinach in salted water until soft – about 3–5 minutes. Mix with the remaining ingredients and season well.

Apples for duck legs

This recipe is for baked apples which I like to eat with the duck legs on page 214 and the red cabbage on page 226. They are also very nice with roast pork or alongside some sausages. And you can even have them as a dessert with Vanilla Custard (see page 142) — just omit the salt and add more sugar, to taste.

SERVES 4 AS A SIDE DISH

4 Cox's apples (or a similar medium-sweet variety)

25g butter

1 tablespoon caster sugar

• salt

Preheat the oven to 180°C/Gas 4.

Remove a thin sliver from the base of each apple; this enables them to sit upright in the baking tin. Rub their skins with plenty of butter then add a sprinkling of sugar.

Line a baking tin with non-stick baking paper and place the apples inside it with a splash of water in the base of the tin. Season the apples with a very small pinch of salt.

Place the tin in the oven and roast for about 20 minutes, basting every so often with the cooking liquor, until the flesh is soft and the skin is bursting and golden. If you feel that the apples are burning before they are becoming soft, add some more water to the tin; this moisture helps them steam a little while they bake.

Apfelküchlein

In a small village high up in the Swiss Alps there is a little 'mountain shed' which serves some of the most delicious food I have so far encountered, including aelplermakkaroni, a sort of mac 'n' cheese baked with apples, Raclette cheese, smoked ham and potatoes; steinpilzsuppe, a hearty mushroom soup with a pastry dome baked on top of the individual soup bowls which you have to break through to get to the soup, resulting in mushroom-soaked nuggets of buttery pastry. And amongst other wondrous delights, for dessert they serve apfelküchlein (apple beignets), sparkling with cinnamon sugar and drenched in warm 'vanilla sauce'. If you really want to go all out, accompany this with a little glass of Poire William or another eau de vie of your choice.

SERVES 6 GENEROUSLY FOR PUDDING

400g	plain flour
3	teaspoons caster sugar
1½	teaspoons salt
450ml	milk
3	eggs
50g	butter, melted
750ml	sunflower oil
8	medium apples, peeled, cored and sliced into rings 1cm thick
200g	cinnamon sugar (caster sugar mixed with 3 teaspoons ground cinnamon)
•	Vanilla Custard (see page 142), warmed, to serve

Sift the flour, sugar and salt into a large mixing bowl. Gradually start to whisk the milk and eggs into one side of the bowl, then the butter, incorporating it slowly into the flour. Leave the batter to sit, covered, in a warm place for about 30 minutes.

Heat the sunflower oil in a very large saucepan or pot, ensuring that the level of the oil does not go higher than a third of the way up the side of the pan. This point is vital as boiling hot oil is obviously very dangerous and if the pan is not big enough, when the apples are dropped in to it, the oil could rise up over the sides of the pan, flowing on to the open flame and cause a fire. This may sound dramatic but it really is a point worth stressing.

You can test the oil is at the right temperature by dropping a spoonful of batter in to the oil; it will fizz and turn furiously on contact with the oil if it is hot enough.

Dip the apples into the batter, coating them generously, then drop them in batches into the hot oil. When you dip your apples in the batter, the mixture should be thick enough to stick to the fruit and hardly drop off. If it slips off, you may need to add a couple more tablespoons of flour to the mixture. The smaller the batches, the quicker the apples will cook and the crispier and more delicious they will be to eat.

When they are golden brown on one side, turn them over with a pair of tongs or a fork and when they are coloured on both sides, remove them to a tray covered with plenty of kitchen paper. Spread them out and leave them to drain well. Cover them in cinnamon sugar and serve hot with warm vanilla custard. My absolute favourite!

Ricotta, lemon, polenta teacakes

This is a lovely, light and fresh cake, which is based on a fantastic recipe that I learned at The River Café. When blood oranges are in season, I like to peel them and slice them into segments, which I caramelise a little, serving them with this cake and a large dollop of crème fraîche. Note that this recipe is gluten-free.

MAKES 7 TEACAKES

125g caster sugar

110g soft butter

- zest of 3½ lemons plus juice of 1½ lemons

100g whole blanched almonds, finely ground in a food processor

3 eggs, separated

50g polenta flour

½ teaspoon salt

½ vanilla pod, split in half, seeds scraped out with a knife

75g fresh ricotta (buffalo milk ricotta is great too)

75g crème fraîche (mascarpone is fine too)

Preheat the oven to 150°C/Gas 2. Line 7 miniature loaf tins (10 x 5 x 3cm) with non-stick baking paper.

Beat the sugar and butter until pale and creamy. Add the lemon zest, almonds, egg yolks, polenta flour, salt and vanilla seeds. In a separate bowl, mix the ricotta, crème fraîche and lemon juice. Add this to the rest of the mixture.

Whisk the egg whites in a very clean bowl until they form soft peaks. Fold one third of the egg whites into the ricotta mixture until the mixture is well combined, then fold in the remaining two thirds as gently as you can manage. Divide the mixture between the loaf tins and bake for 35–40 minutes or until the cakes are coming away from the sides of the tins and a skewer inserted into their centre comes out clean.

Banana, lemon sorbet

SERVES 4–6

1kg	very ripe bananas
200ml	lemon juice
350g	caster sugar

Blend all of the ingredients in a food processor. Churn in an ice-cream machine or transfer to a shallow freezer-proof container and follow the instructions on page 133.

Apple, cinnamon, oat crumble

SERVES 8–10

300g	butter, plus 30g for the apples
500g	soft light brown sugar
1.8kg	Cox's apples, peeled, cored and roughly chopped into 2cm cubes
1	vanilla pod, split in half, seeds scraped out with a knife
280g	plain flour
150g	medium porridge oats
1	teaspoon ground cinnamon
1	teaspoon salt
•	Vanilla Custard (see page 142), to serve

Preheat the oven to 200°C/Gas 6.

In a saucepan heat the 30g of butter with 50g of the sugar and add the apples and vanilla seeds. Cook gently for about 10–15 minutes, until the apples are soft and there is no excess liquid in the pan.

Meanwhile, in a large mixing bowl, rub the remaining sugar, flour and 300g of butter together between your fingers until you have a fairly heavy crumb. Fold in the oats, cinnamon and salt and mix well.

Place the apples in a roasting tin or ceramic baking dish and sprinkle over the crumble topping. Bake in the oven for 15–20 minutes or until golden brown and crisp. Serve hot with the vanilla custard.

Beetroot, dill, apple

This is particularly nice with charcuterie or smoked fish. Sharp, tangy and crisp, it is also well suited to fattier cuts of meat, such as pork chops.

SERVES 4 AS A SIDE SALAD

4   raw red beetroot, peeled and grated

6   Cox's apples, peeled and grated

1   heaped tablespoon Dijon mustard

2   tablespoons sherry vinegar

4   tablespoons extra-virgin olive oil

4   tablespoons finely chopped dill

•   salt and freshly ground black pepper

Mix all the ingredients in a bowl then check for seasoning. Leave to stand for an hour or so to allow the flavours to come out.

Rosemary, Sage, Thyme, Bay

Pork, Bay, Watercress 105

Swiss Chard, Rosemary, White Bean
     Soup 108

Veal, Bay, Carrots 114

Beans, Sage, Garlic 117

Salt Beef, Bay, Thyme 119

Venison, Bay, Prunes 122

Bean, Rosemary, Ham Hock Soup 123

Veal Chop, Sage, Lemon 124

Pork, bay, watercress

SERVES 8–10 AS A MAIN COURSE

2kg	pork cheeks
3	medium cooking chorizo sausages
4	country-style pork sausages
5	rashers streaky bacon, roughly diced
½	tablespoon fennel seeds
½	tablespoon caraway seeds
2	fennel bulbs, cut into quarters
500g	tinned peeled plum tomatoes
5	garlic cloves, peeled
2	large red onions, finely chopped
½	head of celery, roughly chopped
2	bay leaves
½	rosemary branch
250ml	apple juice
750ml	chicken stock

- salt and freshly ground black pepper
- cooked cannellini beans (see page 117), to serve
- Aioli (see page 153), to serve
- watercress, to serve

Preheat the oven to 225°C/Gas 7½.

In a pot large enough to encompass all the ingredients, put the pork cheeks, half of each type of sausage, the bacon, fennel seeds, caraway seeds, fennel, tomatoes, garlic, onion, celery, bay, rosemary, apple juice and chicken stock. Season generously with pepper but cautiously with salt – there is salt already in the bacon and sausages.

Place a cartouche over the top. A cartouche is the name for a disk of baking parchment cut to fit snugly over the contents of a pot (usually it sits on the liquid, if there is enough of it). Its primary aim is to reduce evaporation, prevent a skin from forming and keep the components submerged. Place a lid on the pot and cook in the oven for 2½–3 hours, or until the pork cheeks can be easily broken up with a fork.

Continues overleaf

Continued from page 105

In the meantime, fry the remaining sausages in a pan and chop roughly. When the braise in the pot is ready, remove the sausages which cooked in the liquid and replace them with the freshly fried ones; this seems pernickety but it is very agreeable to have the nicely browned sausages in the final dish as opposed to the discoloured and largely tasteless (most of the flavour has left the sausages during the cooking and gone wonderfully into the stewing liquid) boiled sausages. Serve in a large bowl ladled over cannellini beans and topped with a large dollop of aioli and plenty of watercress.

Swiss chard, rosemary, white bean soup

This soup is great for using up the contents of the vegetable drawers when things are not at their freshest. If you don't have Swiss chard stalks, don't worry, just use more of the other vegetables or add something of your own choice.

MAKES 6–8 HEARTY PORTIONS

3 red onions, finely diced

4 garlic cloves, finely chopped

1 leek, white part only, roughly chopped

½ head of celery, roughly chopped

3 carrots, roughly chopped

2 parsnips, roughly chopped

1 head celeriac, peeled and roughly chopped

200g new potatoes, roughly chopped

4 tablespoons roughly chopped Swiss chard stalks

1 tablespoon very finely chopped rosemary

5 tablespoons roughly chopped parsley leaves

3 tablespoons olive oil, plus some good stuff for pouring over the soup at the end

½ bunch cavolo nero, stalks removed, leaves roughly chopped

500g cooked cannellini beans (see page 117, they must be very soft and beginning to disintegrate, so cook them for about 15 minutes longer than you might if you were cooking them to eat as a side dish on their own)

• salt and freshly ground black pepper

In a large heavy-bottomed saucepan, fry the onion, garlic, leek, celery, carrot, parsnip, celeriac, potatoes, Swiss chard stalks, herbs and a little salt in the olive oil over a medium heat. Cook for 25–30 minutes until very soft, stirring occasionally. Add the cavolo nero and cook for a further 15 minutes. Finally, add the cannellini beans and 200ml of boiling water and simmer, covered, for a further 20 minutes. The soup is meant to be thick but add some more boiling water if you feel that it is too thick. Check for seasoning and serve with a generous glug of your best olive oil.

Veal, bay, carrots

I like to put some different mustards, chutneys, pickles or mustard fruits on the table for people to have with the meat.

SERVES 6 AS A MAIN COURSE

- <u>8</u> osso bucco
- <u>2</u> tablespoons salt
- <u>2</u> bay leaves
- <u>5</u> carrots, peeled and roughly chopped
- <u>2</u> red onions, peeled and halved
- <u>2</u> leeks, washed, outer leaves removed
- <u>1</u> head garlic, skin on, halved and sliced horizontally through the middle
- <u>1</u> bunch flat-leaf parsley, stalks separated, leaves finely chopped, plus extra, to serve
- • freshly ground black pepper
- • extra-virgin olive oil, to serve

Place the osso bucco, salt, bay leaves, carrots, onions, leeks, garlic and parsley stalks in a large pot. Cover with water and bring to the boil, then simmer gently for about 1 ½ hours until the meat is very tender. Remove the osso bucco then pass the liquid through a sieve. Reserve the boiled carrots and any white parts of the leeks. Check the broth for seasoning. Roughly chop the boiled carrots and leeks in to small pieces and return to the broth.

Ladle the broth into bowls and sprinkle with the chopped parsley leaves. Serve the osso bucco on a separate platter with some of the hot broth poured over the top, some extra-virgin olive oil drizzled over and plenty more chopped parsley.

Beans, sage, garlic

SERVES 6–8 AS A SIDE DISH

500g	dried borlotti or cannellini beans, soaked in plenty of water for at least 12 hours
1	bunch sage, tied with cooking string
1	red chilli
1	head garlic, skin on, sliced horizontally through the middle
2	plum tomatoes (tinned is fine)
100ml	olive oil, plus some more of your finest to finish
•	salt and freshly ground black pepper

Place the drained beans, sage, chilli, garlic and tomatoes in a large saucepan and cover with cold water. The water level should be 2.5cm above the beans. Add the olive oil. Place a lid on top and bring the pan to the boil. Reduce the heat and simmer for about 1 hour, or until the beans and their skins are soft. You may need to top the pan up with water during this time; the beans should always have at least an inch of water above them in which to boil freely. For best results add a good pinch or 2 of salt about 5 minutes before you think that the beans are cooked. Turn off the heat and allow them to sit in their liquid for at least 15 minutes. Check for seasoning and make any adjustments slowly, allowing the salt and pepper to dissolve and be absorbed in to the beans. Add some olive oil to finish.

Salt beef, bay, thyme

How you serve this and how many it serves is entirely up to you. I make it to have it in the fridge, like a cured ham. It sits in its cooking liquor and I whip it out for sandwiches and snacks as required. It will keep about 5–7 days in the fridge in an airtight container.

SERVES ROUGHLY 6–8 (BUT SEE ABOVE)

2kg brined beef brisket (this should be available from a good butcher)

6 bay leaves

4 tablespoons coriander seeds

1 tablespoon fennel seeds

1 head garlic, halved horizontally through the middle

1 red onion, quartered

1 teaspoon dried chilli

1 rosemary branch

½ bunch fresh thyme

3 celery sticks

1 tablespoon black peppercorns

Rinse the brisket in cold water a couple of times to remove any excess brine.

Place all the ingredients in a large pot and cover with water. The water level should come to at least 2.5cm above the top of the pot's contents. Bring to the boil then reduce the heat and simmer for 3–3½ hours or until the meat is very tender.

Venison, bay, prunes

SERVES 4–6 AS A MAIN COURSE

1kg diced venison haunch

10 rashers streaky bacon, roughly chopped

8 dried prunes

9 garlic cloves, peeled

3 bay leaves

1 teaspoon juniper berries

1 head celeriac, peeled and roughly chopped

4 carrots, roughly chopped

2 leeks, roughly chopped

2 cooking apples, roughly chopped

500ml red wine

300ml water

For the sauce:

250g frozen mixed summer berries

250ml apple juice

Preheat the oven to 250°C/Gas 9. Place all of the ingredients for the stew in a large pot. Cover and roast in the oven for about 2¼ hours. Remove the lid and roast for a further 15 minutes.

Meanwhile, make the sauce by heating the berries in a saucepan with the apple juice. Simmer until the sauce thickens and the berries are very soft.

Bean, rosemary, ham hock soup

SERVES 4–6

250g   borlotti beans

250g   cannellini beans

1   medium ham hock

4   carrots, peeled

½   head celery

2   red onions, skin on, halved

2   heads garlic, skin on, halved
     horizontally through the middle

2   bay leaves

½   bunch flat-leaf parsley

2   sprigs rosemary

2   teaspoons black peppercorns

2   tablespoons white wine vinegar

3   tablespoons olive oil, plus a little extra
     to serve

•   salt

•   flat-leaf parsley, roughly chopped, to
     serve

In a large pot, soak the beans overnight in plenty of water with all of the ingredients except the olive oil.

The next day, adjust the water so you have at least 5–8cm of cold water above the beans before you start cooking.

Over a medium heat, bring the liquid to the boil and simmer for at least 2 hours or until the beans are very soft. Take out the ham hock, rosemary, parsley and onions, garlic, celery and carrots and set aside. Discard the celery, parsley and rosemary. Release the onions from their outer skins with your fingers; they should slip out very easily. Do the same with the garlic cloves. Take out half the beans and blend them in a food processor with the olive oil, onions and garlic until smooth.

Check the seasoning and return the purée to the rest of the soup. Pull the ham off the bone and add it to the soup. Stir well. If the soup is too thick, you can loosen it with some boiling water.

Serve in bowls with the roughly chopped parsley and some more olive oil.

Veal chop, sage, lemon

The size of chop that I have suggested might feel like a lot of meat but I find that thick chops cook really nicely, giving you a lovely golden surface, crispy fat and meat that's still pink inside. They also look quite impressive served up on a plate with perhaps only a lemon wedge to accompany them. And finally, it is always great to have some meat left over — I slice it finely and eat it cold with capers and green beans, slathered in tuna mayonnaise.

SERVES 2

2   thick veal chops (ask your butcher to cut you 3.5cm T-bone chops; these have both sirloin and fillet meat and are so incredibly delicious)

4   tablespoons olive oil, plus some of your finest olive oil to pour over the chops at the end

1   lemon, halved

1   tablespoon fresh sage leaves

•   salt and freshly ground black pepper

•   Potatoes, Lemon, Oregano (see page 80), to serve

Preheat the oven to its maximum — approximately 250°C/Gas 9. Remove the veal from the fridge at least one hour before cooking.

Pat the chops dry with kitchen paper then season generously with salt. Heat an ovenproof frying pan large enough to encompass both chops (or two frying pans if needs be) until it is very hot but not smoking. Pour in the oil then immediately place the veal chops in the pan. Brown the meat until a dark golden on one side, about 6 minutes. Flip the chops over and remove the pan from the heat. Squeeze over the lemon juice (throw the lemon skins into the pan as well) and add the sage leaves. Add a final glug of your best olive oil then roast in the oven for about 8 minutes. I like my veal to be quite pink and juicy. To check for doneness, make a small incision into the meat with a knife.

Allow the chops to rest for a good 10 minutes. Season with pepper and squeeze out the roasted lemon halves for any remaining juice. Plate the chops, spoon over the pan juices and serve with a side plate of lemon potatoes.

The
Fridge Door

Eggs, Milk

Chocolate Ice Cream 132

Fresh Mint Ice Cream 134

Gingerbread Ice Cream 138

Earl Grey Ice Cream 140

Josh's Morning Smoothie 141

Vanilla Custard 142

Rhubarb, Vanilla, Custard 144

Meringues 1 148

Meringues, Cream, Strawberries 150

Meringues 2 152

Aioli 153

Chocolate ice cream

SERVES 6–8

1½	tablespoons cocoa powder
225ml	full-fat milk
750ml	double cream
1	vanilla pod, split in half, seeds scraped out with a knife
9	egg yolks
175g	caster sugar
40g	dark chocolate (70 per cent cocoa solids)
120g	dark chocolate (50 per cent cocoa solids), plus 40g, roughly chopped, for folding through at the end

Make a paste with the cocoa powder by adding a couple of tablespoons of the milk to the cocoa and stirring vigorously. When you have a smooth, lump-free paste, heat this in a saucepan with the rest of the milk and stir for 5–10 minutes.

Meanwhile, in a separate pan, heat the cream, vanilla pod and seeds over a medium heat. Once warm, add the cocoa milk, stirring from time to time to ensure that the milk does not catch at the bottom. When the liquid comes to a boil reduce the heat and simmer for a further 15 minutes.

Meanwhile, in a mixing bowl, beat the egg yolks and sugar until pale. Pour a little of the hot milk mixture into the egg yolks and whisk furiously for a moment – this is to get the eggs used to the heat of the milk without scrambling them; 'tempering' the eggs, to be more precise – and then immediately pour the eggs into the saucepan. Over a low heat gently stir the mixture back and forth with a wooden spoon until the custard is thick enough to coat the back of the spoon and a line drawn with your finger across it holds its shape. Pour the custard through a fine sieve into a shallow freezer-proof container. Add both types of chocolate and stir them into the mixture – they should melt easily. Allow to cool then churn in an ice-cream machine or freeze in the container, following the instructions below. Before the ice cream is entirely frozen, stir in the roughly chopped chocolate.

If you are using an ice-cream machine, follow the manufacturer's instructions. To hand-churn, whip the container out of the freezer every 30 minutes or so and beat the mixture vigorously with a wooden spoon or whisk. Repeat this process for 3–4 hours until the ice cream is almost completely frozen. During the freezing process, ice crystals will begin forming as the ice cream turns from a liquid to a solid. So as to get as smooth a result as possible, it is necessary to continuously break up any large ice crystals and spread them as evenly as possible through the mixture. This process is labour-intensive but essential for making ice cream without an electric machine. These machines churn the mixture continuously as it freezes and generally produce a smoother, more consistent result. I would say that a small worktop ice-cream maker with a removable bowl and electric paddle is ideal for home use if you are regularly going to be making ice cream. With these machines you remove the metal bowl and keep it in the freezer until use. There are also machines that have a freezing unit contained within them so the mixture is poured directly into the machine, frozen and churned at once, however, these are costly and cumbersome.

Fresh mint ice cream

SERVES 6–8

750ml	double cream
225ml	full-fat milk
2	large bunches fresh mint, tied together with cooking string
1	vanilla pod, split in half, seeds scraped out with a knife
9	egg yolks
175g	caster sugar

In a heavy-bottomed saucepan, heat the cream, milk, mint and vanilla pod and seeds over a medium heat, stirring from time to time to ensure that the milk does not catch at the bottom. When the liquid comes to a boil reduce the heat and simmer for a further 15 minutes.

Meanwhile, in a mixing bowl, beat the egg yolks and sugar until pale. Pour a little of the hot milk and cream into the egg yolks and whisk furiously for a moment (see page 132 for why you need to do this), then immediately pour the eggs into the saucepan. Over a low heat gently stir the mixture back and forth with a wooden spoon until the custard is thick enough to coat the back of the spoon and a line drawn with your finger across it holds its shape. Pour the custard through a fine sieve into a shallow freezer-proof container, then fish out the bunches of mint and put them into the container. Allow to cool and sit in the fridge for at least 24 hours; 48 hours is ideal.

Remove the mint leaves, then churn the custard in an ice-cream machine or put the container in the freezer and follow the instructions on page 133.

Gingerbread ice cream

This is a good way of using up any less-than-fresh leftover Gingerbread (see page 200).

SERVES 6–8

750ml	double cream
225ml	full-fat milk
3	cinnamon sticks
1	vanilla pod, split in half, seeds scraped out with a knife
9	egg yolks
175g	caster sugar
200g	Gingerbread (see page 200), pulsed in a food processor to medium/fine crumbs

In a heavy-bottomed saucepan, heat the cream, milk, cinnamon sticks and vanilla pod and seeds over a medium heat, stirring from time to time to ensure the milk does not catch at the bottom. When the liquid comes to a boil reduce the heat and simmer for a further 15 minutes.

Meanwhile, in a mixing bowl, beat the egg yolks and sugar until pale. Pour a little of the hot milk and cream into the egg yolks and whisk furiously for a moment (see page 132 for why you need to do this), then immediately pour the eggs into the saucepan. Over a low heat gently stir the mixture back and forth with a wooden spoon until the custard is thick enough to coat the back of the spoon and a line drawn with your finger across it holds its shape. Pour the custard through a fine sieve into a shallow freezer-proof container. Fish out the cinnamon sticks and return them to the container. Allow to cool and store in the fridge for 24–48 hours. Remove the cinnamon sticks, then churn the custard in an ice-cream machine or put the container in the freezer and follow the instructions on page 133. Before the ice cream is entirely frozen, stir in the ginger cake crumbs.

Earl Grey ice cream

I began to make this ice cream when I had the good fortune to meet Henrietta Lovell, founder of the Rare Tea Company. Whilst this ice cream is delicious with any Earl Grey tea, her variety, infused with bergamot oil from the south of Italy, makes it uniquely aromatic and almost savoury in its flavour.

SERVES 6–8

225ml	full-fat milk
750ml	double cream
20g	Earl Grey tea leaves
1	vanilla pod, split in half, seeds scraped out with a knife
9	egg yolks
175g	caster sugar

Put the milk, cream and Earl Grey tea leaves in a large container and allow to infuse for at least 24 hours, ideally 48 hours.

In a heavy-bottomed saucepan, heat the tea mixture and vanilla pod and seeds over a medium heat, stirring from time to time to ensure that the milk does not catch at the bottom. When the liquid comes to a boil reduce the heat and simmer for a further 15 minutes.

Meanwhile, in a mixing bowl, beat the egg yolks and sugar until pale. Pour a little of the hot milk mixture into the egg yolks and whisk furiously for a moment (see page 132 for why you need to do this), then immediately pour the eggs into the saucepan. Over a low heat gently stir the mixture with a wooden spoon back and forth until the custard is thick enough to coat the back of the spoon and a line drawn with your finger across it holds its shape. Pour the custard through a fine sieve into a shallow freezer-proof container. Allow to cool then churn in an ice-cream machine or put the container in the freezer and follow the instructions on page 133.

Josh's morning smoothie

MAKES 1.5 LITRES

300g	blueberries
800ml	almond milk
3	bananas
150g	strawberries
5	tablespoons agave syrup
2½	tins lychees in syrup, drained (total drained weight of 500g)

In a food processor or blender, pulse the blueberries with one tablespoon of the almond milk. Add the bananas then the rest of the ingredients. Blend until smooth, then sieve and chill.

Vanilla custard

GENEROUSLY SERVES 10 SPOONED OVER BOWLS OF CRUMBLE OR ANYTHING ELSE YOU FANCY...

750ml   double cream

225ml   full-fat milk

1   vanilla pod split in half, seeds scraped out

9   egg yolks

175g   caster sugar

In a heavy-bottomed saucepan, heat the cream, milk and vanilla pod and seeds over a medium heat, stirring from time to time to ensure that the milk does not catch on the bottom. When the liquid comes to a boil reduce the heat and simmer for a further 15 minutes.

Meanwhile, in a mixing bowl, beat the egg yolks and sugar until pale. Pour a little of the hot milk and cream into the egg yolks and whisk furiously for a moment (see page 132 for why you need to do this), then immediately pour the eggs into the saucepan. Over a low heat gently stir the mixture back and forth with a wooden spoon, until the custard is thick enough to coat the back of the spoon and a line drawn across it with your finger holds its shape. Pour the custard through a fine sieve into a suitable jug or container. Serve warm or cold according to preference.

Rhubarb, vanilla, custard

SERVES 4 AS A PUDDING

<u>12</u> sticks champagne rhubarb (about 800g), sliced into 5cm lengths

<u>1</u> vanilla pod, split in half, seeds scraped out

<u>225g</u> caster sugar

<u>2</u> oranges, halved

• Vanilla Custard (see page 142) or ice cream, to serve

Preheat the oven to 180°C/Gas 4.

In a bowl, mix the rhubarb, vanilla seeds and sugar with your hands. Squeeze over the oranges and mix well. Put the rhubarb in a large roasting tin, separating out the pieces so that they are flat on the tin and not piled on top of each other. Cover the tin with foil and roast for about 15 minutes.

Remove the foil and carefully press the rhubarb with your finger or a wooden spoon – it should be soft to touch but still retain its shape; once removed from the oven it will cook a little further in the tin. Serve warm or cold with custard, ice cream or anything you fancy!

Meringues 1

MAKES 15 MEDIUM-SIZED MERINGUES

250g   caster sugar

1   vanilla pod, split in half, seeds scraped out

4   egg whites (125g)

Preheat the oven to 120°C/Gas ½.

In a mixer or with a hand whisk, whisk the sugar, vanilla seeds and egg whites until they form either stiff peaks or shapes that look like ducks' beaks, or when you put a spoon into the mixture and pull it upwards, the mixture holds a crest shape like a wave! Using a tablespoon, spoon the mixture onto a lined baking sheet in circles measuring about 8cm wide. Bake for 1½ hours. They should be a very pale peach colour, crisp on the outside and chewy on the inside.

Meringues, cream, strawberries

This is my version of Eton Mess, which is an English pudding traditionally containing strawberries, crushed meringue and cream. While researching its origins I discovered a rather curious theory: that the Eton Mess first came into being when a meringue dessert was sat on by a Labrador en route to a picnic at Eton college and the squashed 'mess' of meringue, cream and strawberries was what was salvageable. All I can think is that it must have been a very unusual Labrador because if it had been my dog there would have been nothing salvageable other than the fasteners of the picnic basket.

SERVES 6 AS A PUDDING

250g	double cream, chilled
50g	icing sugar
1	vanilla pod, split in half, seeds scraped out
2	large punnets strawberries, chilled then hulled
2	punnets raspberries, chilled
1	batch Meringues 1 (see page 148)

Whisk the cream, icing sugar and vanilla seeds until they form soft peaks.

In a large bowl, roughly break up a few meringues, then top with a little cream, some berries, and follow this procedure until you have a full bowl of pudding. Serve while everything still feels chilled.

Meringues 2

These meringues are made with coconut and are sometimes known as coconut kisses. The coconut gives them a denser, heavier texture than meringues made just with egg whites.

MAKES 12 MEDIUM-SIZED MERINGUES

250g	caster sugar
1	vanilla pod, split in half, seeds scraped out
4	egg whites (125g)
100g	desiccated coconut

Preheat the oven to 120°C/Gas ½.

In a mixer or with a hand whisk, whisk the sugar, vanilla seeds and egg whites until they form either stiff peaks or shapes that look like ducks' beaks, or when you put a spoon into the mixture and pull it upwards, the mixture holds a crest shape like a wave! Gently fold in the coconut. Using a tablespoon, spoon the mixture onto a lined baking sheet in circles measuring about 8cm wide. Bake for 50 minutes – they will be off-white and fairly dense in texture.

Aioli

This garlicky mayonnaise is great with fish, chicken and raw vegetables. It is also lovely in a sandwich.

SERVES 8 AS A GARNISH

2 egg yolks, at room temperature

• pinch of salt

½ garlic clove, mashed up

• lemon juice, to taste

500ml your best extra-virgin olive oil

Put the egg yolks and salt into a bowl with the garlic and roughly a tablespoon of lemon juice. Start to whisk, continuing for about 1 minute, then slowly trickle in the olive oil while continuously whisking. If the consistency starts to look lumpy or greasy (in technical terms, it is starting to split), I add just a tablespoon of boiling water. This should make the emulsion more stable and enable you to carry on adding more oil. In general, three things cause an emulsion to split: firstly if the mayonnaise gets too hot or the eggs are very cold and the oil very warm to begin with; secondly if you add the olive oil too quickly while whisking; thirdly if you add too much oil. If you want to understand the science behind the process in more detail there is plenty of literature on the internet. I personally split every aioli I tried to make for the first month or two when I worked at The River Café. I found the paragraph on emulsions in Harold McGee's book *On Food and Cooking* very helpful.

Cream,
Sour cream

Yoghurt 156

Aubergine, Lemon, Yoghurt 158

Carrot, Yoghurt, Cumin Soup 159

Yoghurt, Mint, Cucumbers 162

Yoghurt Ice Cream 164

Apricots, Vanilla, Yoghurt 165

Bircher Muesli 166

Muesli 168

Granola 172

Horseradish, Crème Fraîche, Lemon 174

Leeks, Cream, Fennel 175

Celeriac, Crème Fraîche, Mustard 176

Yoghurt

This is a recipe inspired by The Moro Cookbook. *I have increased the ratio of cream to make it thicker as I generally use this as a topping for stew or in sauces.*

MAKES 1.5 KG

2 litres full-fat milk

400ml double cream

150g live yoghurt

Bring the milk to the boil in a large pot. Reduce the heat and simmer for about 20–30 minutes until you have reduced the volume of milk by a third. Stir from time to time to ensure that the milk does not burn on the bottom.

Pour in the cream and allow to cool. The mixture should cool only up to a point where it is bearable to hold your finger in the liquid for 10 seconds without it burning you. Stir in the yoghurt, pour the mixture through a sieve and cover the bowl with cling film. Leave to stand in a warm place, like an airing cupboard, for 8–12 hours. It is good to cover the bowl with an extra blanket or cloth.

Aubergine, lemon, yoghurt

Using smoked salt is a great way of achieving the smokiness that you get when you roast aubergines slowly over a barbecue.

SERVES 6–8 AS A SIDE DISH

4 aubergines, spiked several times with a fork and wrapped tightly in foil

6 tablespoons best olive oil

2 garlic cloves, finely sliced

• couple of large pinches smoked salt

1 teaspoon ground cumin

• pinch dried chilli

5 tablespoons Greek-style yoghurt (minimum 10 per cent fat)

2 tablespoons finely chopped mint

• juice of 1 lemon

• freshly ground black pepper

Preheat the oven to 200°C/Gas 6.

Roast the aubergines in the oven for about 2 hours, until the flesh is completely soft; like apple compote in consistency. Scrape out the flesh and allow to drain in a sieve for 30 minutes.

Heat the olive oil in a frying pan. Fry the garlic with some salt until a light golden in colour, then add the aubergine, cumin and chilli. Cook for about 10 minutes then remove from the heat and stir in the yoghurt, mint, lemon and black pepper. Check the seasoning and chill in the fridge until serving.

Carrot, yoghurt, cumin soup

SERVES 4

<u>6</u> garlic cloves, finely chopped

<u>1</u> bunch flat-leaf parsley, leaves only, roughly chopped

½ teaspoon crushed dried chilli

<u>3</u> tablespoons olive oil

<u>20</u> carrots, finely diced or pulsed in a food processor

2½ tablespoons honey

<u>1</u> teaspoon ground ginger

½ teaspoon ground nutmeg

<u>1</u> tablespoon ground cumin

<u>500ml</u> milk

<u>250ml</u> double cream

<u>250ml</u> water

- salt and freshly ground black pepper
- coriander leaves, to serve
- nigella (black onion) seeds, to serve
- Greek-style yoghurt, to serve

In a large heavy-bottomed saucepan, fry the garlic, parsley and chilli in the oil over a medium heat until the garlic starts to turn a light golden. Add the carrots, honey, ginger, nutmeg and cumin.

Cook the carrots over a medium heat, stirring the pan from time to time for about an hour, until they are very soft and sweet. Add the milk, cream and water and continue to cook for a further 10 minutes, then check the seasoning. Pour half the contents of the saucepan into a food processor or blender and blend until smooth, then return this to the pan. Serve the soup sprinkled generously with coriander leaves, nigella seeds and a dollop of yoghurt.

Yoghurt, mint, cucumbers

This is how I make what I have tasted and known to be tzatziki in Greece. By other names and in different consistencies, the Cypriots, Bulgarians and Turks (to name a few) have different variations of and occasions for this dish. If you have an aversion to raw garlic, or a new date to kiss, this is also lovely without the garlic and perhaps even more aromatic.

SERVES 4–6 AS A MAIN COURSE

500g Greek-style yoghurt (or any 10 per cent fat strained yoghurt – do not use reduced fat varieties; sheeps' yoghurt is a lovely alternative if you can get hold of it)

5 small Greek cucumbers (if you can find them) or ¾ regular cucumber, halved lengthways and cut into medium–fine slices

6 tablespoons olive oil

• juice of 1 lemon

3 tablespoons finely chopped mint

3 tablespoons roughly chopped dill

1 garlic clove, peeled and mashed to a paste with the back of a knife and some salt

• salt and freshly ground black pepper

In a bowl, mix all of the ingredients together with some salt and pepper. Allow to sit for a few minutes and then check the seasoning. Chill until serving.

Yoghurt ice cream

SERVES 4

1kg	homemade Yoghurt (see page 156) or any Greek-style yoghurt (10 per cent fat)
200g	caster sugar
1	vanilla pod, split in half, seeds scraped out with a knife

Mix the contents together then churn in an ice-cream machine or transfer to a shallow container, place in the freezer and follow the instructions on page 133.

Apricots, vanilla, yoghurt

I really like this for a luxurious breakfast with homemade Granola (see page 172).

SERVES 4 AS A GENEROUS TOPPING

125g	caster sugar
½	vanilla pod, split in half, seeds scraped out
5	ripe apricots, torn in half, stone removed
•	homemade Yoghurt (see page 156)

In a saucepan heat the sugar and vanilla pod and seeds with 3 tablespoons of water. Allow to bubble on a high heat for 5 minutes. Add the apricots and cook in the hot sugar for a further 5 minutes, until they still hold their shape but are releasing liquid and the skins are starting to burst. Remove from the heat and place a lid on the pan. Allow the apricots to stand for a further 10–15 minutes. Remove the vanilla pod then serve warm or cold on top of the yoghurt.

Bircher muesli

I find Bircher muesli much easier to digest in the morning than regular muesli as soaking the oats seems to reduce greatly the sensation of them swelling and expanding inside one's stomach. The oats absorb almost all of the initial liquid and the final consistency is that of a very thick porridge.

SERVES 4

200g	porridge oats
120g	raisins
80g	dried figs, roughly chopped
60g	ground almonds
40g	toasted coconut chips (unsweetened)
1	tablespoon wheat germ
1	tablespoon golden linseed
2	tablespoons blanched hazelnuts
2	tablespoons pumpkin seeds
2	tablespoons walnut halves
1	cinnamon stick
•	small pinch of salt
1	teaspoon ground cinnamon
4	medium apples (Cox's or Braeburn are nice and tangy for this), skin on, grated
500ml	milk
200ml	Greek yoghurt or cream
1	tablespoon honey

Combine all the ingredients and leave in the fridge for at least 6 hours.

Muesli

SERVES 4–6

200g   porridge oats

120g   raisins

80g   dried figs, roughly chopped

60g   ground almonds

40g   toasted coconut chips (unsweetened)

2   tablespoons blanched hazelnuts

2   tablespoons pumpkin seeds

2   tablespoons walnut halves

1   tablespoon wheat germ

1   tablespoon golden linseed

1   teaspoon ground cinnamon

•   small pinch of salt

Combine all the ingredients and serve with milk or spoon on top of yoghurt.

Granola

This recipe is based on the honey granola recipe from the Rose Bakery cookbook, Breakfast, Lunch, Tea. *I love Rose Carrarini's book, which is full of beautiful recipes and pictures; it's comfort food with a capital 'C'.*

MAKES APPROXIMATELY 2KG

225g	honey
100g	light brown sugar
1½	teaspoons salt
2	teaspoons vanilla extract
1	teaspoon ground cinnamon
125ml	sunflower oil
125ml	water
400g	rolled oats
250g	desiccated coconut
175g	whole roasted hazelnuts
175g	whole blanched almonds
100g	walnuts
200g	raisins or sultanas
1	vanilla pod, split in half
350g	dried apricots, roughly chopped
50g	sesame seeds

Preheat the oven to 200°C/Gas 6.

In a saucepan, heat the honey, sugar, salt, vanilla extract, cinnamon, oil and water until they come to the boil, then remove from the heat.

Put the oats, 200g of the coconut, 125g of the hazelnuts and the almonds in a bowl. Add the honey and cinnamon mixture and stir very well. Pour the oats into a roasting tray and place in the oven for approximately 50 minutes–1 hour. It is crucial that you stay near the oven so that you can stir the granola every 10–15 minutes to ensure that the oats are evenly toasted and that the nuts on the top don't have a chance to burn. This feels a bit like a labour of love – and it is – but it is worthwhile. When the oats are nicely golden brown, remove from the oven and allow to cool; they will turn ever so slightly browner on cooling so don't overdo it in the oven! Finally, stir in the walnuts, raisins, vanilla pod, apricots, sesame seeds and the remaining coconut and hazelnuts. Serve with milk or spoon on top of yoghurt.

Horseradish, crème fraîche, lemon

SERVES 6–8 AS A GARNISH FOR A MEAT MAIN COURSE OR SPREAD IN A ROAST BEEF SANDWICH

50g   peeled fresh horseradish, finely grated then very finely chopped

200ml   crème fraîche

2   tablespoons red wine vinegar

1   tablespoon lemon juice

•   salt and freshly ground black pepper

Mix all of the ingredients together in a bowl. Season and allow to stand for a few minutes before tasting and re-seasoning.

Leeks, cream, fennel

This is good as a side dish with roast chicken or fish but I actually prefer it as a wintry main course with a green salad and some hot bread.

SERVES 4 AS A SIDE DISH OR 2 AS A MAIN COURSE

4 garlic cloves, peeled

• juice of 1½ lemons

3 leeks, green part removed, cut into 1cm-thick diagonal pieces

4 fennel bulbs, halved then quartered, tops and outer leaves removed

150g white crustless bread (ciabatta is good)

200g grated Parmesan

2 tablespoons thyme leaves

6 tablespoons olive oil

450ml double cream

• salt and freshly ground black pepper

Preheat the oven to 180°C/Gas 4.

Put the garlic and two thirds of the lemon juice in a large pot of boiling salted water. Cook the leeks, then remove them and cook the fennel in the same water until very soft. The leeks will take about 10 minutes and the fennel about 15 – but check to make sure they are very soft.

In a food processor, pulse the bread until you have coarse breadcrumbs. In a large bowl, mix the breadcrumbs with the cheese, thyme, some salt, plenty of pepper and the olive oil.

Once the vegetables are cooked, allow them to drain well but do not throw out the cooking liquid – this is very important for this dish. Place 300ml of the cooking liquor back in the pot and return it to the heat. Add the cream and reduce the liquid until it is quite thick – about 10 minutes. Check the seasoning then add the remaining lemon juice.

In a roasting dish (about 25cm long and 10cm deep) place the vegetables, pour over the cream and top with the breadcrumbs. Bake in the oven for 15–20 minutes, until the breadcrumbs are golden brown and the creamy sauce is bubbling up over the sides.

Celeriac, crème fraîche, mustard

This is my version of the French dish, celeriac remoulade. It is lovely on a platter with cold cuts or served in a ciabatta with some boiled chicken (see page 32) or roast ham hock (see page 41) and Little Gem lettuce.

SERVES 4–6 AS A SMALL SIDE DISH

250g celeriac, peeled and finely grated

250g crème fraîche

½ tablespoon red wine vinegar

1 tablespoon wholegrain mustard

• salt and freshly ground black pepper

Mix all the ingredients in a bowl with some salt and pepper. Check the seasoning and allow to sit for a few minutes before checking again.

The Dry Stores Cupboard

Nutmeg, Cinnamon, Ginger

Tomato, Cinnamon, Garlic 182

Borlotti, Cinnamon, Tomato 183

Green Beans, Cinnamon, Tomato 184

Leek, Nutmeg, Cavolo Nero 186

Celeriac, Nutmeg, Cream 187

Chestnut, Nutmeg, Bacon Soup 188

Pears, Cinnamon, Star Anise 192

Carrot, Cinnamon, Walnut Cake 194

Gingerbread 200

Banana, Cinnamon, Pineapple Bread 202

Tomato, cinnamon, garlic

This tomato sauce is wonderful with all kinds of summer vegetables and pulses, particularly long string beans and garden peas. The addition of cinnamon and honey finds inspiration in the tomato sauces which I have tasted in Greece, most usually slathered over baked aubergines, meatballs or white beans, and topped with mizithra cheese.

SERVES 6–8 AS AN ACCOMPANYING SAUCE

5 tablespoons olive oil, plus extra for serving

3 red onions, very finely sliced

2 garlic cloves, finely sliced

¼ teaspoon crumbled dried red chilli

1 teaspoon ground cinnamon

2 tablespoons honey

1kg tinned plum tomatoes

• salt and freshly ground black pepper

In a wide-rimmed heavy-bottomed saucepan, heat the olive oil and fry the onion with the garlic and a generous pinch of salt over a medium heat until the onions are very soft but not brown – about 20 minutes. Add a pinch of pepper, the chilli, cinnamon, honey and the tomatoes. Cook, stirring regularly on a medium heat for about 50 minutes or until the sauce is a dark red in colour and any excess tomato liquid has evaporated. Check the seasoning and serve with some extra olive oil on top.

Borlotti, cinnamon, tomato

As well as a side dish, these beans would make a lovely easy supper on a piece of toast rubbed with garlic, topped with crumbled ricotta and plenty of freshly chopped parsley.

SERVES 6–8 AS A SIDE DISH OR 4 AS A MAIN ON TOAST

1   batch of Tomato, Cinnamon, Garlic sauce (see opposite)

500g   warm cooked borlotti beans (see page 117)

3   tablespoons roughly chopped flat-leaf parsley

Heat the tomato sauce then place in a bowl with the warm borlotti beans and parsley.

Green beans, cinnamon, tomato

SERVES 6–8 AS A SIDE

500g green string or runner beans, ends removed

1 batch of Tomato, Cinnamon, Garlic sauce (see page 182)

3 tablespoons roughly chopped parsley

• salted ricotta or a similar firm cheese, such as manouri or feta, for grating (optional)

• olive oil, to serve

In a large pot of boiling water, blanch the beans until soft. Heat the tomato sauce in a pan and add the cooked beans to the sauce. Cook together on a medium heat until the beans lose most of their shape and split apart. They will be very soft, very tomatoey but still distinguishable as beans; this takes about 10 minutes. Remove from the heat and stir in the chopped parsley. If you are serving this as a side, finish with a generous grating of salted ricotta and some olive oil. If you are serving this as a garnish for meat or fish, perhaps omit the cheese.

Leek, nutmeg, cavolo nero

A great lunch dish served with a large piece of sourdough rubbed with garlic.

SERVES 2 AS A SIDE DISH WITH MEAT OR FISH OR 1 AS LUNCH

50g butter

3 garlic cloves, finely sliced

3 leeks, finely sliced

2 handfuls cavolo nero, stalks removed, blanched until tender (if you can't get hold of cavolo, use the outer leaves of Savoy cabbage)

1 teaspoon ground nutmeg

1 handful roughly chopped flat-leaf parsley

In a saucepan, heat the butter and cook the garlic slices until golden brown. Add the leeks and fry on a low heat until soft, about 15 minutes. Roughly chop the blanched cavolo nero and stir into the leeks. Add the nutmeg. Cook for a further 5 minutes. Serve garnished with plenty of parsley.

Celeriac, nutmeg, cream

This is a good side dish for a Sunday roast or a topping for pies, especially game pie.

SERVES 6 AS A SIDE DISH

2	heads celeriac, peeled and cut into 2.5cm squares
250ml	double cream
50g	butter
1	teaspoon freshly grated nutmeg
•	salt and freshly ground black pepper

Place the celeriac in a large pot of boiling salted water and boil until extremely soft – this takes at least 30 minutes so be patient; if the celeriac is not soft enough, this dish will not be nice. Drain the celeriac well and return it to the hot pot. With a potato masher, mash the cream, butter and nutmeg into the celeriac. It is up to you how crushed you want your celeriac. Check the seasoning and serve immediately.

Chestnut, nutmeg, bacon soup

SERVES 6–8

25g	butter
3	tablespoons olive oil
12	rashers streaky bacon, roughly chopped
1	leek, finely diced
1	head celery, finely diced
3	heads celeriac, peeled, finely diced
½	bunch parsley, stalks removed, roughly chopped, plus a little extra to serve
3	red onions, finely diced
1	bay leaf, spine removed, pounded with a little salt in a pestle and mortar to a fine dust
1½	tablespoons ground nutmeg
2	juniper berries, roughly crushed
5	garlic cloves, finely chopped
300g	cooked, peeled chestnuts (you can buy these vacuum-packed), roughly chopped
250ml	double cream
1 litre	chicken stock
•	salt and freshly ground black pepper

In a large saucepan, heat the butter and olive oil over a low–medium heat and gently fry the bacon, leek, celery, celeriac, parsley, onion, bay, nutmeg, juniper, garlic and a little salt until very soft – about 1 hour. Add the chestnuts and cook for a further 15 minutes. Finally add the cream and chicken stock and simmer gently for 10 minutes. Check the seasoning, adding some pepper and a little more chopped parsley to serve.

I delight in opening the fridge door, having a mosey in the vegetable drawers, catching a whiff of an overly ripe cheese and deciding what feast I am going to create.

Pears, cinnamon, star anise

SERVES 6 AS A PUDDING

200g caster sugar

6 pears (I like to use Williams pears if I can get my hands on them but most pears will do), peeled, halved, core removed

1 cinnamon stick

• pinch of black pepper

8 star anise

250ml red wine

• warm Vanilla Custard (see page 142) or cream, to serve

In a wide-rimmed saucepan, heat the sugar gently over a low heat and place the pears in cored-side down. Add the cinnamon, black pepper and star anise. When the sugar has melted, add the red wine and place a cartouche (a circle of greaseproof paper or baking parchment that fits snugly inside the pan) gently over the pears. Simmer the pears for approximately 25 minutes, or until the pears are nice and soft and the cooking liquid has reduced to a centimetre from the base of the pan. Remove the greaseproof paper and increase the heat. Allow the pears to colour and become slightly stuck to the bottom of the pan. Flip the pears over before they become too stuck. Turn off the heat and add 150ml of water to the pan to loosen the sugar mixture, then leave it to heat through.

Serve the pears with warm vanilla custard or cream and a little of the cooking liquor spooned over the top.

Carrot, cinnamon, walnut cake

MAKES 1 LOAF CAKE

165g   carrots, finely grated

165g   plain flour

165g   soft light brown sugar

130g   tinned pineapple, finely chopped

40g   desiccated coconut

50g   walnuts, finely chopped, plus a large handful of extra halves, to decorate

¼   teaspoon salt

½   tablespoon vanilla extract

1¾   teaspoons ground cinnamon

¾   teaspoons ground nutmeg

½   teaspoon baking powder

1   teaspoon bicarbonate of soda

100ml   corn oil

2   medium eggs

For the icing:

150g   cream cheese, at room temperature

65g   butter, at room temperature

50g   icing sugar

½   teaspoon vanilla extract

Preheat the oven to 180°C/Gas 4. Line a 900g loaf tin with baking paper.

Combine all the cake ingredients in a bowl. Mix well. Spoon the mixture into the tin and bake for about 50 minutes–1 hour. You may have some left over – if so, spoon this into muffin cases and bake for 20 minutes in the same oven. To test for doneness, insert a skewer into a cake (or muffin) – it should come out clean. Leave to cool in the tin.

For the icing, the cream cheese and butter must have been left out at room temperature while you make the cake – this step is important for a smooth icing. In a mixer or by hand, mix the cheese, butter and sugar together, then stir in the vanilla extract.

Spread over the icing and crumble walnut halves over the top.

Gingerbread

MAKES 1 LOAF CAKE

125g	butter
150ml	golden syrup
150ml	full-fat milk
½	teaspoon ground cinnamon
½	teaspoon ground nutmeg
2	teaspoons ground ginger
•	small pinch of salt
100g	soft light brown sugar
1½	teaspoons baking powder
1½	teaspoons bicarbonate of soda
250g	plain flour
1	egg
75g	caster sugar
½	punnet redcurrants
225ml	double cream
½	vanilla pod, seeds scraped out
50g	icing sugar

Preheat oven to 170°C/Gas 3½. Line a 900g loaf tin with baking paper.

Melt the butter and golden syrup in a saucepan. Take off the heat and add the milk. Put the spices, salt, light brown sugar, baking powder and bicarbonate of soda and flour in a bowl. Whisk the butter mixture into the flour then beat in the eggs. Spoon the mixture into the tin. Bake for about 50 minutes or until a skewer inserted into the centre comes out clean. Cool in the tin.

Heat 40g of the caster sugar in a pan with a splash of water. Simmer until the sugar has dissolved and you have a light syrup – about 10 minutes. Dip the redcurrants, with stalks attached, into the syrup and roll in the remaining caster sugar. Place on a baking sheet and put in the fridge to set.

Whip the cream with the vanilla seeds and icing sugar until thick. Spread over the cake and sprinkle with the sugared redcurrants.

Banana, cinnamon, pineapple bread

MAKES 1 LOAF CAKE

165g	extremely over-ripe bananas (about 3 medium bananas), mashed with a fork, plus one extra banana for the topping
165g	plain flour
150g	soft light brown sugar, plus 1 extra tablespoon for the topping
130g	tinned pineapple (drained weight), finely chopped
40g	desiccated coconut
50g	walnuts, finely chopped
¼	teaspoon salt
½	tablespoon vanilla extract
1¾	teaspoon ground cinnamon
¾	teaspoons ground nutmeg
½	teaspoon baking powder
1	teaspoon bicarbonate of soda
90ml	corn oil
2	medium eggs
1	tablespoon porridge oats

Preheat the oven to 180°C/Gas 4. Line a 900g loaf tin with baking paper.

Combine all the ingredients except the oats in a bowl. Mix well then spoon into the lined tin. Slice the remaining banana into diagonal slivers and layer on top of the cake. Sprinkle the oats over the top of the cake followed by the tablespoon of brown sugar. Bake for about 50 minutes–1 hour. To test for doneness, insert a skewer into the cake – it should come out clean. Cool in the tin.

Selecting just a few 'fruits of the fridge' with which to concoct a meal is the real adventure in cooking.

Coriander
seed,
Fennel seed,
Caraway
seed

Josh's Virgin Mary 208

Lamb, Coriander Seed, Garlic 212

Aubergine, Coriander Seed, Currants 213

Duck Leg, Fennel Seed, Cider 214

Pork Cheek, Coriander Seed, Barley 218

Lamb, Coriander Seed, Prunes 222

Brussels Sprouts, Caraway Seed, Bacon 225

Red Cabbage, Caraway Seed, Apple 226

Potatoes, Fennel Seed, Garlic 228

Josh's Virgin Mary

My friend Josh, who works as a bartender in some of London's top restaurants, designed this Virgin Mary for a Mexican restaurant. I am in awe of his skills. Mixing drinks – alcoholic and non-alcoholic – has never come easily to me, and in fact I have been known to make the worst Pimm's on record – quite a feat given the simplicity of its components! I don't drink very often and so I have chosen to include this recipe for a Virgin Mary. Often I make this if I have friends over and don't feel like joining them in a glass of wine but don't want plain water. Josh suggests that the combination of the Cholula hot sauce and smoked chipotle make this meaty and thick to drink so it can be enjoyed on its own without a nibble. Of course if you want to make this into a Bloody Mary, he recommends using 50ml vodka to 125ml of the Virgin Mary for a nice balance.

MAKES 2 LITRES

2 litres plain tomato juice

125ml Worcestershire sauce

7 drops Cholula hot sauce

15 drops Tabasco chipotle sauce

½ jalapeno pepper, seeded

½ red chilli, seeded

1 tablespoon coriander leaves

1 garlic clove

1 large celery stick

• juice of ½ lemon

Place 500ml of the tomato juice in a food processor or blender with the remaining ingredients and blend until very smooth. Stir in the remaining tomato juice. Serve chilled garnished with extra celery, if you like.

Lamb, coriander seed, garlic

Almost every Sunday morning when I was younger, I woke to the smell of lamb shanks roasting in the oven. Onions, garlic and coriander permeated the walls and I would arrive pyjama-clad in the kitchen. Especially in winter, on those dark and icy mornings, waking up and seeing the glow of the light in the oven obscured only by the large lamb shank pot was comfort with a capital C. This is also great the next day, perhaps in ciabatta with some Greek-style yoghurt and fresh coriander.

SERVES 6 AS A MAIN COURSE

<table>
<tr><td>1</td><td>lamb shoulder (about 2.5kg) or 6 lamb shanks</td></tr>
<tr><td>4</td><td>tablespoons olive oil</td></tr>
<tr><td>2</td><td>garlic heads, skin on, sliced horizontally through the middle</td></tr>
<tr><td>4</td><td>large red onions, skin on, quartered</td></tr>
<tr><td>3</td><td>large bunches coriander, washed and roughly chopped</td></tr>
<tr><td>2</td><td>large handfuls coriander seeds, roughly pounded in a pestle and mortar</td></tr>
<tr><td>750ml</td><td>red wine</td></tr>
<tr><td>1</td><td>litre water</td></tr>
<tr><td>•</td><td>salt and freshly ground black pepper</td></tr>
</table>

Preheat the oven to 200°C/Gas 6.

Season the lamb all over with plenty of salt (but no pepper at this stage as it will burn). Heat a large, wide-rimmed pot over a high heat until very hot but not smoking, add the olive oil then immediately add the lamb and brown until golden on all sides.

Pour away the fat then put the lamb back in the pot with the garlic, onion, fresh coriander and seeds. Pour over the wine then enough water so that the liquid comes three quarters of the way up the lamb. Season with a little more salt and pepper.

Place in the oven and cook for 3½ hours until the lamb can easily be pulled away from the bone with a fork.

Aubergine, coriander seeds, currants

SERVES 6–8 AS A SIDE DISH

6   tablespoons olive oil

3   red onions, finely chopped

15 garlic cloves, finely chopped

6   aubergines, chopped into 1cm cubes

1kg chopped tinned tomatoes

3   cinnamon sticks

2   tablespoons freshly ground coriander
    seeds

1   tablespoon ground cumin

1   tablespoon freshly crushed black
    peppercorns

•   rind of 2 lemons, finely sliced

1   tablespoon raisins

1   tablespoon currants

•   salt and freshly ground black pepper

1   bunch coriander or parsley, roughly
    chopped, to serve

If time allows, it is best to cook this the night before and leave it to sit overnight to allow the flavour to develop.

In a heavy-bottomed saucepan, fry the onion and garlic over a medium heat in 2 tablespoons of the oil for about 20 minutes, until soft. Add the aubergine and some salt and fry for a further 10 minutes. Add the tomatoes, cinnamon sticks and all of the remaining ingredients except the fresh coriander and cover with a lid. Simmer very slowly, stirring regularly – it has a habit of sticking – for at least 1½ hours. I try not to put too much olive oil in at this stage as the tomatoes should provide enough liquid, but you can add a small glass of water. When it's ready, the aubergine flesh, raisins and currants should be completely soft and most of the liquid will have evaporated. Check the seasoning: aubergines can take a lot of salt. Serve with a generous amount of coriander, or parsley if you prefer, along with the remaining 4 tablespoons of oil stirred through the dish.

Duck leg, fennel seed, cider

SERVES 4 AS A MAIN COURSE

4	duck legs
6	tablespoons olive oil
2	tablespoons fennel seeds
2	red onions, quartered
1	head garlic, skin on, sliced in half horizontally through the middle
750ml	semi-sweet/sweet cider (Normandy or Cidre de Bretagne is the best if you can get hold of it)
•	salt and freshly ground black pepper

Preheat the oven to 180°C/Gas 4.

Season the duck legs with plenty of salt. In a wide-rimmed heavy-bottomed saucepan, heat the olive oil. When the oil is hot, brown the duck legs skin-side down in the pan until the skin is crisp and golden. Remove the pan from the heat and discard the excess oil.

Return the duck legs to the pan, seasoning them with the fennel seeds and some black pepper. Add the onions and garlic and pour over the cider. The liquid level should come halfway up the sides of the meat. If you need more liquid, add water, apple juice or more cider. Cover the pan with a cartouche (see page 105) and a tight-fitting lid. Cook for about 2 hours in the oven or until the meat can be pulled easily away from the bone with a fork. Turn the oven up to its maximum – about 250°C/Gas 9, remove the lid and cartouche and roast for a further 15–20 minutes until the skin is crisp.

Pork cheek, coriander seed, barley

These pork cheeks are cooked until they are extremely soft, then roasted again in the oven with coriander seed and seasoning until they are very crisp. It is best served just warm; the pork straight from the oven mixed through the barley, which has already been allowed to cool and dry a little, plus the fresh herbs and leaves. In this way the salad remains vibrant and, along with the barley, offers a cool contrast to the hot, crisp pork cheek. For an excellent lunch on the go, pack some tortilla wraps with the pork mixture along with plenty of yoghurt.

SERVES 10 AS A MAIN COURSE

2kg	pork cheeks
4	tablespoons whole coriander seeds, roughly pounded in a pestle and mortar
2	fennel bulbs, quartered
500g	tinned peeled plum tomatoes
5	rashers streaky bacon, roughly diced
5	garlic cloves, peeled
2	large red onions, finely chopped
½	head celery, roughly chopped
2	bay leaves
1	bunch coriander
250ml	apple juice
750ml	chicken stock
10	tablespoons Yoghurt, Mint, Cucumbers (see page 162), to serve
•	salt and freshly ground black pepper

Preheat the oven to 225°C/Gas 7½.

Put all of the ingredients in a pot large enough to encompass the entire pork cheek braise, reserving 2 tablespoons of coriander seeds to finish. Season generously with pepper but cautiously with salt – there is salt in the bacon. Place a cartouche over the top (see page 105) then put a lid on the pot and cook in the oven for 2½–3 hours, or until the pork cheeks are meltingly soft.

While the pork is in the oven, boil the barley in plenty of salted water for about 25 minutes, or until soft but still retaining a bite. Drain the barley and mix with the watercress, herbs, olive oil, lemon and some pepper.

For the barley:

250g   barley, rinsed in cold running water for
       several minutes

2   bunches watercress, stalks removed,
    roughly chopped

8   tablespoons coriander leaves

5   tablespoons mint leaves

6   tablespoons finely chopped parsley

4   tablespoons olive oil

•   juice of 1 lemon

When the pork is ready, remove from the pot and shake off any excess liquid. Roughly shred the meat and place on a baking tray. Check the seasoning, then add the remaining 2 tablespoons of crushed coriander seeds. Add a drop of olive oil and plenty of pepper. Place the pork back in the oven, uncovered, for 15–20 minutes, turning the meat from time to time to ensure that all sides get crispy. Finally, toss the pork with the barley and serve with the Yoghurt, Mint, Cucumbers.

Lamb, coriander seed, prunes

This is a warming spiced stew based on a dish that my mother used to cook for my father to remind him – on drizzly London days – of the Bushveld and Cape Town where he was born. It is her version of a South African curry from the Malay community of the Western Cape and, having never asked her for the actual recipe, my version is one further step removed from its beginnings.

MAKES 6 LARGE BOWLS OF STEW

2kg	diced lamb leg (or if you are at the butcher, ask what they would recommend from their available stock for braising)
3	tablespoons olive oil
4	red onions, roughly chopped
5	garlic cloves, peeled
½	teaspoon ground cinnamon
½	teaspoon ground ginger
2	tablespoons coriander seeds, pounded until fine in a pestle and mortar
1	teaspoon crumbled dried chilli
8–10	medium prunes, stones removed, roughly chopped
1½	tablespoons honey
500g	tinned chopped tomato
800ml	chicken stock
•	boiled chickpeas (see page 52) or rice, to serve
•	homemade Yoghurt (see page 156) or any Greek-style yoghurt (10 per cent fat), to serve
1	bunch coriander, leaves only, to serve
•	salt and freshly ground black pepper

Preheat the oven to 250°C/Gas 9.

Season the lamb generously with salt (not pepper at this stage as it will burn). Heat a large, wide-rimmed saucepan and when hot but not smoking, add the oil, then immediately add the lamb and brown it in batches in the oil. Aim for a nice golden brown on each piece. Remove the lamb to a bowl then discard any oil left in the pan.

In the same saucepan, add the onion, garlic, cinnamon, ginger, coriander seed, chilli, prunes, honey and a splash of water. Allow these to cook over a medium heat for about 20 minutes, until soft.

Into a pot large enough to encompass the whole stew, pour the lamb, tomatoes, stock and contents of the saucepan. Put a lid on the pot and place in the oven for 1½–2 hours. When the curry is ready the meat should be very tender and the sauce quite thick. Serve with boiled chickpeas or rice with a dollop of yoghurt and the coriander leaves scattered over generously.

Brussels sprouts, caraway seed, bacon

SERVES 4 AS A SIDE DISH

450g   Brussels sprouts, peeled, trimmed, an 'X' cut into the base of each

30g   butter

4   garlic cloves, finely sliced

4   tablespoons roughly chopped parsley

6   rashers smoked streaky bacon, cut into 1cm strips

2   teaspoons caraway seeds

•   salt

Cook the Brussels sprouts in plenty of boiling salted water until soft – about 15 minutes – then drain well.

In a saucepan, melt the butter over a medium heat and fry the garlic with some salt until light golden in colour. Add half the parsley and the bacon and fry for a further 10 minutes until the bacon is starting to colour. Add the caraway seeds and finally the Brussels sprouts. Increase the heat and fry the sprouts for about 5 minutes. Finish with the remaining parsley.

Red cabbage, caraway seed, apple

I like this with baked duck legs (see page 214) or with quickly fried pork sausages, mustard and a chunk of hot bread.

SERVES 6–8 AS A SIDE DISH

4 tablespoons olive oil

3 garlic cloves, peeled, finely sliced

6 rashers smoked streaky bacon, finely diced

1 tablespoon caraway seeds

3 semi-sweet apples (Cox's apples are good), peeled, cored and finely diced

1 red cabbage, halved, core removed, finely sliced

2 tablespoons caster sugar

4 tablespoons red wine vinegar

2 tablespoons butter

• salt and freshly ground black pepper

In a large heavy-bottomed saucepan, heat the oil and fry the garlic until very light golden brown in colour. Add the bacon and caraway seeds and fry for a further 5 minutes. Add the apple, cabbage, sugar and vinegar. Cook on a low heat for about 40 minutes, stirring from time to time to prevent the cabbage from catching. When the cabbage is very soft – you do not really want any bite to it at all – and a bit caramelised, add the butter and stir well. Check the seasoning and serve hot.

Potatoes, fennel seed, garlic

If I can get my hands on them I really like using Ratte, Rosevale or Pink Fir Apple potatoes, but if not regular baby new potatoes will do. These potatoes go nicely with the duck legs (see page 214) and the Red Cabbage, Caraway Seed, Apple recipe (see page 226).

SERVES 6 AS A SIDE DISH

2kg	new potatoes (see above)
3	tablespoons olive oil
30g	butter
2	garlic cloves, very finely sliced
1½	tablespoons finely ground fennel seeds (ground in a pestle and mortar or spice grinder if you have one)
•	salt and freshly ground black pepper

Boil the potatoes in plenty of salted water until only just soft, about 15 minutes, although it can take longer depending on your potatoes, so just keep testing until you're happy they're ready. It is important that the potatoes are not too soft or they will fall apart in the frying pan; not that this is too much of a problem – you will just end up with more of a potato and fennel hash rather than individual elegant sautéed potatoes. Drain the potatoes and leave to cool.

When the potatoes are almost completely cold, slice them in half. Heat a frying pan and when hot but not smoking, add the oil, then immediately place the potatoes in the pan skin-side up. Add plenty of salt. Leave the potatoes to brown and crisp – this may take longer than you think, have patience! When they are crisp and deep golden in colour, flip them over and reduce the heat. Add the butter, garlic slivers, fennel seed and some black pepper. Continue frying slowly until the garlic is a gentle nutty brown.

Anchovies,
Dried
mushrooms,
Capers,
Mustard,
Rose water,
Orange flower
water,
Vinegar

Ox Cheek, Porcini, Tomato 234

Barley, Thyme, Porcini Soup 240

Celeriac, Anchovy, Mustard 242

Walnut Dressing, Salad Leaves 244

Onion Jam 245

Potatoes, Dill, Capers 246

Mr Abraham's Tomato Sauce 248

Lentils, Dill, Mustard 249

Salsa Verde 253

Pear, Lemon, Rose Sorbet 255

Carrots, Orange Blossom Water, Lemon 256

Blood Oranges, Mint, Rose Water 257

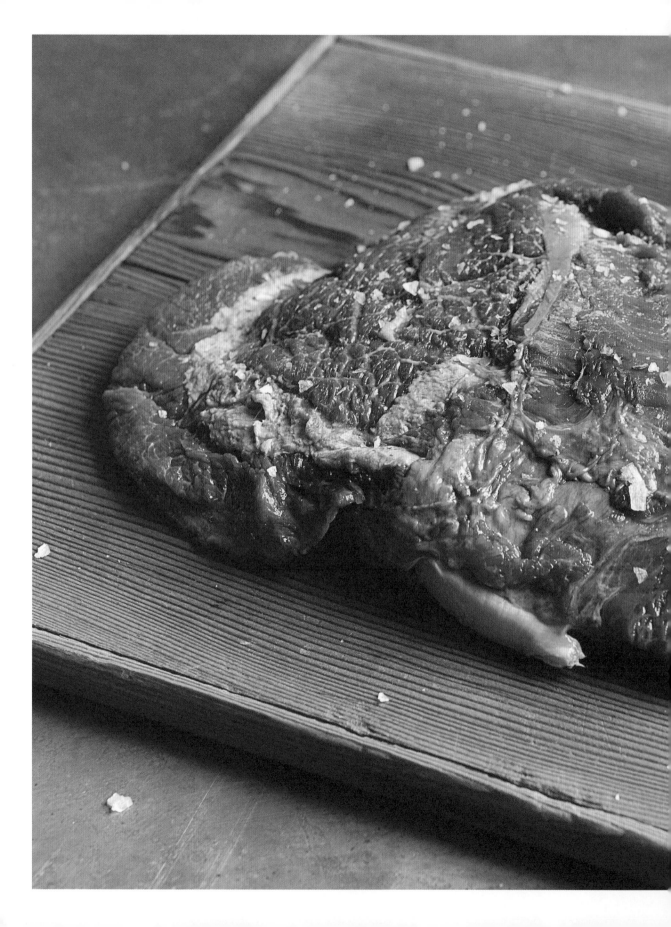

Ox cheek, porcini, tomato

Serve this stew with some bread and a green salad or for something more hearty, with pearl barley and plenty of roughly chopped parsley.

MAKES 6–8 BOWLS OF STEW

2	tablespoons dried porcini
4	tablespoons olive oil
2kg	ox cheek (cut into roughly 5 x 2.5cm pieces)
6	rashers streaky bacon, roughly chopped.
500ml	chicken stock
300g	tinned chopped tomatoes
375ml	red wine
5	garlic cloves, peeled
2	red onions, roughly chopped.
2	carrots, roughly chopped
½	head celery, roughly chopped
2	bay leaves
1	rosemary branch
2	juniper berries
1	tablespoon thyme leaves
•	pinch of dried chilli
•	salt and freshly ground black pepper

Preheat the oven to 225°C/Gas 7½.

Start by soaking the porcini. Place in a bowl and cover with boiling water. Cover the bowl with cling film. Leave for 15–20 minutes, then drain. It's a good idea to reserve the soaking liquor and freeze it in cubes to use in stocks, soup or sauces.

Heat the olive oil in a heavy-bottomed pot large enough to encompass the whole stew. Season the ox cheek generously with salt then add to the pot and brown in the oil – about 2 minutes on each side (you might need to do this in batches). Remove the ox cheek and pour away any excess oil, then return the meat to the pot with some pepper and all of the other ingredients. Put a lid on the pot and place in the oven for 2½–3 hours. When the stew is ready the meat will hold its shape but fall gently apart on contact with a fork.

My niece Maebh eating ox cheek.

Barley, thyme, porcini soup

SERVES 8

50g	butter
6	garlic cloves, finely sliced
2	tablespoons thyme leaves
2	red onions, finely diced
2	celery hearts, finely diced
4	leeks, leafy green parts removed, finely diced
4	tablespoons dried porcini, rehydrated in 1 litre boiling water, drained and finely chopped (keep the water used to rehydrate the porcini)
1.2kg	potatoes, peeled and finely diced
½	head celeriac, finely diced
600ml	chicken stock or water
250g	pearl barley, rinsed in cold water
250ml	double cream
•	large handful flat-leaf parsley, roughly chopped, plus a little extra to serve
•	salt and freshly ground black pepper

In a saucepan large enough to encompass the entire volume of soup, melt the butter and fry the garlic, thyme, onion, celery, leek and porcini. When soft, add the potato, celeriac, porcini liquid and chicken stock or water to cover. Simmer gently until very soft, about 45 minutes.

In a saucepan, boil the barley in plenty of salted water until tender, about 20 minutes. Drain well.

When the vegetables are soft, take half of them and blend until smooth in a food processor. Return the purée to the pan. Add the cream, chopped parsley and check the seasoning. Add the barley and serve with some extra chopped parsley in each bowl.

Celeriac, anchovy, mustard

This recipe finds inspiration in a dish often served with lamb rump that I have had many times at my favourite local restaurant, Hereford Road. Tom Pemberton and his lovely neighbourhood restaurant are a rock for me in all things food related: an intimate dinner for two, a business lunch, a birthday, a solo meal, it never fails to deliver! If I am having a cosy night in alone, I like very much to have this as a main course, a large steaming bowl of it with perhaps a couple of bitter salad leaves.

SERVES 4 AS A SIDE DISH OR 2 AS A MAIN COURSE

1	head celeriac, peeled and roughly chopped into 2.5cm cubes
5	tablespoons olive oil
3	garlic cloves, finely sliced
3	anchovy fillets
2	large handfuls flat-leaf parsley, roughly chopped
1½	tablespoons Dijon mustard
•	salt

Put the celeriac into a large pot of cold salted water. Bring to the boil and simmer until very tender. This takes quite a while – a good 25 minutes at least, so be patient. Drain, keeping back a little of the cooking liquid.

In a large wide saucepan, heat the oil and fry the garlic slices with a pinch of salt over a medium heat. When the garlic starts to colour, gently add the anchovy fillets; these will dissolve. Add the parsley; this will pop and spit for a while, so stand back. Add the celeriac and the mustard and a splash of the cooking liquid if the celeriac starts to stick/burn to the bottom of the pan or is looking very dry. Cook gently, stirring from time to time, for 20–25 minutes until all the ingredients are combined and you have a very chunky mash.

Walnut dressing, salad leaves

I am never sure what to make of salads hiding all manner of 'trail mix' beneath their leaves; I'm left with the feeling of having ingested starter, main course and dessert all at once – in effect a kind of Willy Wonka Gobstopper. However this salad perhaps a few times a year is really rather enjoyable, especially around Christmas time.

SERVES 6–8 AS A STARTER

- 1 tablespoon Dijon mustard
- 1 tablespoon honey, dissolved in a tablespoon of boiling water
- 200ml walnut oil
- 1 tablespoon sherry vinegar
- 150g pecan nuts, toasted gently in a low oven with a little salt and olive oil
- 4 tablespoons dried cranberries
- baby spinach leaves, enough for 6–8
- salt and freshly ground black pepper

Mix the mustard and honey with a fork, then slowly pour in the walnut oil. Add the vinegar. Season with salt and pepper. Toss the leaves with the nuts and cranberries and spoon over the dressing.

Onion jam

SERVES 2–4 AS A GARNISH

25g   butter

3   tablespoons olive oil

2   large red onions, very finely sliced

2   tablespoons white wine vinegar

2   teaspoons brown sugar

•   salt and freshly ground black pepper

In a saucepan, melt the butter in the olive oil and add the thinly sliced red onions. Fry the onions until they are soft – about 25 minutes, then add the vinegar and sugar.

Cover and cook slowly, checking that the liquid has not evaporated completely – if so, add a couple of teaspoons of water to stop the onions from sticking to the pan and burning.

After 20 minutes or so, the onions should caramelise and become dark and sticky. Check the seasoning. This can be served warm or once cool.

Potatoes, dill, capers

This potato salad is great when eaten on a summer's day, just warm, with a selection of other small salads or some cold meats. I like Cyprus potatoes if I can find them; they are the extremely muddy ones with a very yellow flesh inside. Roseval potatoes are good too. If you can't find either of these, look in your supermarket for ones that are suitable for boiling and mashing, like King Edward or Maris Piper.

SERVES 6 AS A SIDE SALAD

2kg large potatoes, peeled and quartered

8 tablespoons best olive oil, plus extra to serve

2 tablespoons red wine vinegar

1 red onion, very finely sliced

1 round garden lettuce, core removed, roughly chopped.

8 tablespoons chopped dill

2 tablespoons capers, roughly chopped

• salt and freshly ground black pepper

Boil the potatoes in plenty of salted water until soft, about 20 minutes but the timing varies so just keep testing them.

Drain and, while still very hot, return the potatoes to the pan and break them up with a potato masher or fork; you don't want mashed potatoes here, rather some roughly bashed ones.

Add the oil and vinegar, onion and some salt and pepper. Fold in the lettuce, dill and capers. Serve warm with some more olive oil on top.

Mr Abraham's tomato sauce

While my mother's cooking seems to have a somewhat higher profile in this book, I would not want to neglect the skill of my father in the kitchen. A man of few dishes but excellent palate, his food never fails to delight those of the lucky few who have the chance to eat it. Almost always packed with his favoured five ingredients, including garlic, olive oil, red wine, honey and dried chilli in various combinations, his food seems to burst with taste! My birthdays with him as a child centred around his tomato pasta. And every year, when offered the opportunity to try a new dish of his, or perhaps even be so bold as to venture out to a restaurant, I always wanted the same tomato sauce.

SERVES 4 ON PASTA

6	tablespoons olive oil
6	garlic cloves, finely sliced
250g	streaky bacon, finely sliced
•	pinch of dried chilli
2	tablespoons honey
1kg	tinned peeled plum tomatoes, roughly chopped
375ml	red wine
•	salt and freshly ground black pepper
•	your best extra-virgin olive oil, to serve

Heat the olive oil in a saucepan and add the garlic slices. Season generously with salt. Fry until golden brown then add the bacon, chilli, honey and tomatoes. Finally add the wine. Allow the sauce to cook on a low heat for 1 hour, stirring from time to time to ensure that it does not catch on the bottom. Finish with a good glug of extra-virgin olive oil and plenty of cracked black pepper.

Lentils, dill, mustard

SERVES 6 AS A SIDE DISH

500g   Puy lentils

1   head garlic, skin on, halved horizontally through the middle

3   tablespoons Dijon mustard

1½   tablespoons honey

3   tablespoons red wine vinegar

2   tablespoons olive oil

1   bunch dill, finely chopped

•   salt and freshly ground black pepper

In a saucepan of boiling water (don't salt the water), cook the lentils with the garlic until soft – about 45 minutes. Drain and put in a bowl.

In a separate bowl, add the mustard to the honey and vinegar, a little hot water to melt the honey, and the olive oil. Season with salt and pepper and add to the lentils with the dill.

Salsa verde

Everybody seems to make a different salsa verde: more mustard, less anchovy, more mint, more vinegar etc. Often it depends on what you're serving it with, for example it is nicer to add more mustard if the salsa is going with a fatty cut of meat so that it cuts through the grease. The choice of herbs is largely up to you. At The River Café, the herbs changed regularly, with the seasons. In the height of summer, when basil was plentiful, we used a mixture of basil, rocket and parsley. Personally I always like a balance of parsley and mint with a heavier leaning towards mint and plenty of red wine vinegar. Additionally I think it is very important to let the salsa sit for at least ten minutes before checking for final seasoning as the flavours really grow and change after a little while.

I find that it is a great sauce for meat and fish alike as well as a welcome addition to roast vegetables or hard-boiled eggs.

SERVES 6 AS A SAUCE FOR A MAIN DISH

10	tablespoons flat-leaf parsley leaves
10	tablespoons mint leaves
4–5	tablespoons extra-virgin olive oil
5	anchovy fillets
1	tablespoon salted capers, soaked in fresh water for 40 minutes–1 hour then drained
3	tablespoons red wine vinegar
1	tablespoon Dijon mustard
1	garlic clove, mashed with a pinch of salt
½	lemon
•	salt and freshly ground black pepper

Take the largest chopping board and knife that you have. The knife needs to be very sharp or you will end up with bruised rather than finely chopped herbs. Bunch the mint and parsley together into a kind of cigar shape. Slice through the herbs repeatedly until you have very small fragments. This will take about 10 minutes of continuous chopping. If you cannot face the manual labour involved, throw the herbs into a food processor and pulse gently. Take care not to over-chop as you will end up with a purée, and for some reason if the herbs are too fine the end flavour is almost grassy.

Continues overleaf

Continued from page 253

For the next stage, it is important to keep
the vibrant green of the herbs before the
air oxidises them and they turn brown.
Put the herbs into a bowl with the olive oil.
Chop the anchovies and capers together until
fine then add to the herbs. Add the red wine
vinegar and stir well. The vinegar will start
to break down the anchovy fillets. Finally add
the mustard, a pinch of salt and pepper and
the smashed garlic. Allow the salsa verde to sit
for 10 minutes or so, then taste. It may need
a squeeze of lemon, or more mustard or salt.
Just make sure any changes you make to the
seasoning are done slowly, allowing time for
the salt to dissolve.

Pear, lemon, rose sorbet

SERVES 4

225g	caster sugar
125ml	water
450g	very ripe pears, peeled and seeds removed
100ml	lemon juice
1	tablespoon rose water

Heat the sugar with the water in a saucepan for 5–10 minutes until the liquid starts to turn a very light golden colour. Allow to cool.

Purée the pears in a food processor until smooth then add the sugar syrup, lemon juice and rose water. Churn in an ice-cream machine or transfer to a shallow container, place in the freezer and follow the instructions on page 133.

Carrots, orange blossom water, lemon

SERVES 4–6

5 carrots, peeled and coarsely grated (if you have different size holes on your grater, go for a fairly large size; it is nice if the carrots appear coarsely grated)

1 tablespoon roughly chopped dill

1 tablespoon roughly chopped mint

1 tablespoon caster sugar

• juice of 1 lemon

1 tablespoon orange blossom water

100ml olive oil

• salt and freshly ground black pepper

In a large mixing bowl, combine the carrot with the herbs and season with salt and pepper.

In a separate bowl, dissolve the sugar in the lemon juice and add the orange blossom water. Pour the mixture over the carrots then add the olive oil. Mix the carrots thoroughly and check the seasoning. Cover with cling film and place in the fridge to marinate for a couple of hours if time allows. If not, serve immediately.

Blood oranges, mint, rose water

SERVES 4 AS A PUDDING

10 blood oranges, peeled and sliced into thin rounds (regular oranges are fine too)

3 tablespoons mint leaves

1 tablespoon rose water

100ml sirop de gomme (sugar syrup easily obtained from your local supermarket or off-licence) or 4 tablespoons caster sugar dissolved in 100ml boiling water simmered for about 10 minutes then chilled

• homemade Yoghurt (see page 156), to serve

Arrange the orange slices and mint leaves on a large plate. In a bowl, whisk the rose water into the sugar syrup and spoon over the oranges. Cover the plate with cling film and place in the fridge for several hours if time allows, but this isn't essential; you can serve it straight away with the homemade yoghurt.

INDEX

A

aioli 153
almond, granola 172–3
almond milk, Josh's morning
    smoothie 141
anchovy, mustard, celeriac
    242–3
apfelküchlein 88–91
apple
    apfelküchlein 88–91
    beetroot, dill 98–9
    berry sauce 122
    Bircher muesli 166–7
    cinnamon, oat crumble
      95–7
    for duck legs 86–7
    red cabbage, caraway seed
      226–7

apricot
    vanilla, yoghurt 165
    see also dried apricot
aubergine
    coriander seeds, currants
      213
    dill, potatoes 58
    lemon, yoghurt 158
    mint, raisin 56–7
avocado, lemon, coriander 84

B

bacon
    caraway seed, Brussels
      sprouts 225
    chestnut, nutmeg soup
      188–91
    Mr Abraham's tomato sauce
      248
    ox cheek, porcini 234–9

pork, bay, watercress 105–7
pork cheek, coriander seed,
    barley 218–21
red cabbage, caraway seed,
    apple 226–7
venison, bay, prunes 122
banana
    cinnamon, pineapple bread
      202–5
    Josh's morning smoothie 141
    lemon sorbet 94
barley
    coriander seed, pork cheek
      218–21
    thyme, porcini soup 240–1
bases, cooking times 19
basil
    garlic, pine nuts 1 (pesto) 50
    garlic, pine nuts 2 (pesto) 50
    lentil, ramson soup 36
bay
    carrots, veal 112–14
    prunes, venison 122

thyme, salt beef 118–19
watercress, pork
    105–7
beans *see* borlotti bean;
    cannellini bean; green bean
beef *see* salt beef
beetroot, dill, apple 98–9
berry apple sauce 122
Bircher muesli 166–7
blood orange, mint, rose water
    257
blueberry, Josh's morning
    smoothie 141
borlotti bean
    cinnamon, tomato 183
    parsley, bread soup
        47–9

rosemary, ham hock soup
    123
sage, garlic 116–17
bread
    banana, cinnamon,
        pineapple 202–5
    borlotti, parsley soup 47–9
breadcrumb(s), parsley, chicken
    38–40
broth, fennel, parsley, chicken
    34
Brussels sprout, caraway seed,
    bacon 225

C

cabbage *see* red cabbage
cakes
    banana, cinnamon,
        pineapple bread 202–5
    carrot, cinnamon, walnut
        194–5
    gingerbread 196–201
    ricotta, lemon, polenta
        teacakes 92–3
cannellini bean
    rosemary, ham hock soup
        123
    sage, garlic 116–17
    Swiss chard, rosemary soup
        108–9
caper, dill, potato 246–7
caraway seed
    apple, red cabbage 226–7
    bacon, Brussels sprouts 225
carrot
    bay, veal 112–14
    chicken, parsley soup 32–3
    cinnamon, walnut cake
        194–5

orange blossom water, lemon
    256
parsley, honey 26
yoghurt, cumin soup 159–61
cavolo nero, leek, nutmeg 186
celeriac
    anchovy, mustard 242–3
    crème fraîche, mustard
        176–7
    nutmeg, cream 187
chestnut, nutmeg, bacon soup
    188–91
chicken
    lemon, tarragon 81–3
    parsley, breadcrumbs 38–40
    parsley, carrot soup 32–3
    parsley, fennel broth 34
    parsley, green beans 27
chickpea, garlic, paprika 52–3
chocolate ice cream 132–3
cider, fennel seed, duck leg
    214–17
cinnamon
    garlic, tomato 182
    oat, apple crumble 95–7
    pineapple, banana bread
        202–5
    star anise, pears 192–3
    sugar 88–91
    tomato, borlotti 183
    tomato, green beans 184–5
    walnut, carrot cake 194–5
coconut
    Bircher muesli 166–7
    granola 172–3
    meringues 2 152
    muesli 168–71
coriander, avocado, lemon 84
coriander seed
    barley, pork cheek 218–21
    currants, aubergine 213
    garlic, lamb 212

prune, lamb 222–3
courgette, mint, ricotta 66–7
cream
    celeriac, nutmeg 187
    fennel, leek 175
    strawberry, meringues 150–1
cream cheese icing 194–5
crème fraîche
    lemon, horseradish 174
    mustard, celeriac 176–7
crumble, apple, cinnamon, oat
    95–7
cucumber, yoghurt, mint 162–3
cumin, carrot, yoghurt soup
    159–61
currant(s), coriander seeds,
    aubergine 213
custard, vanilla 142–3
    rhubarb 144–7

D

dandelion, parsley, ham hock
    41–3
dill
    apple, beetroot 98–9
    capers, potato 246–7
    Little Gem lettuce, peas
        64–5
    mint, peas 63
    mustard, honey dressing 69
    mustard, lentil 249
    potatoes, aubergines 58
    radish, green leaves 70
    sherry vinegar, tomato
        60–1
dressings
    honey, dill, mustard 69
    walnut, salad leaves 244
dried apricot, granola 172–3

duck leg
    apple for 86–7
    fennel seed, cider 214–17

E

Earl Grey ice cream 140

F

fennel
    broth, parsley, chicken 34
    leek, cream 175
fennel seed
    cider, duck leg 214–17
    garlic, potatoes 228–9
fig
    Bircher muesli 166–7
    muesli 168–71
flat bread, mint, lemon 59

G

garlic
    coriander seed, lamb 212
    fennel seed, potatoes 228–9
    mayonnaise 153
    paprika, chickpea 52–3
    parsley, peppers 19, 24–5
    pine nuts, basil 1 (pesto) 50
    pine nuts, basil 2 (pesto) 50
    sage, beans 116–17
    tomato, cinnamon 182
    tomato, parsley sauce 37
gingerbread 196–201
    ice cream 138–9
granola 172–3
green bean
    chicken, parsley 27
    cinnamon, tomato 184–5
green leaves, dill, radish 70–1

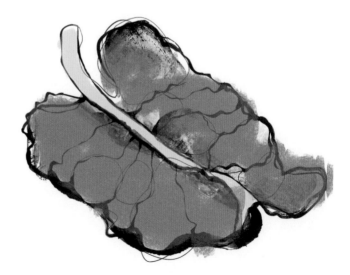

H

ham hock
    bean, rosemary soup 123
    parsley, dandelion 41–3
hazelnut, granola 172–3
honey
    carrots, parsley 26
    dill, mustard dressing 69
    granola 172–3
horseradish, crème fraîche,
    lemon 174

I

ice cream
    chocolate 132–3
    Earl Grey 140
    fresh mint 134–7
    gingerbread 138–9
    yoghurt 164
icing, cream cheese
    194–5

J

jam, onion 245
Josh's morning smoothie 141
Josh's Virgin Mary 208–11

K

khobez, mint, lemon 59
kohlrabi, mint, smoked
    paprika 62

L

lamb
    chops, mint, lemon 74–5
    coriander seed, garlic 212
    coriander seed, prunes
      222–3
leek
    cream, fennel 175
    nutmeg, cavolo nero 186
lemon
    banana sorbet 94
    carrot, orange blossom water
      256
    coriander, avocado 84
    horseradish, crème fraîche
      174
    mint, khobez 59
    mint, lamb chops 74–5
    oregano, potatoes 80
    polenta, ricotta teacakes
      19, 92–3
    rose, pear sorbet 255
    sage, veal chop 124–5
    tarragon, chicken 81–3
    watercress, spinach 85
    yoghurt, aubergine
      158
lentil
    dill, mustard 249
    ramsons, basil soup 36
Little Gem lettuce
    green leaves, dill, radish
      70–1
    peas, dill 64–5
lychee, Josh's morning
    smoothie 141

M

mayonnaise, garlic 153
meringue
    1 148–9
    2 152
    cream, strawberry 150–1
mint
    cucumbers, yoghurt 162–3
    dill, peas 63
    fresh, ice cream 134–7
    lemon, khobez 59
    lemon, lamb chops 74–5
    raisin, aubergine 56–7
    ricotta, courgette 66–7
    rose water, blood orange 257
    smoked paprika, kohlrabi 62

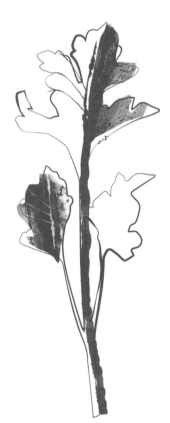

Mr Abraham's tomato sauce 248
muesli 168–71
    Bircher 166–7
mustard
    anchovy, celeriac 242–3
    celeriac, crème fraîche
        176–7
    dill, lentil 249
    honey, dill dressing 69

N

nutmeg
    bacon, chestnut soup 188–91
    cavolo nero, leek 186
    cream, celeriac 187

O

oat, apple, cinnamon crumble
    95–7
onion jam 245
orange *see* blood orange
orange blossom water, lemon,
    carrot 256
oregano, lemon, potatoes 80
ox cheek, porcini, tomato
    234–9

P

paprika
    garlic, chickpea 52–3
    see also smoked paprika
parsley
    bread, borlotti soup 47–9

breadcrumbs, chicken
    38–40
carrot, chicken soup 32–3
chicken, fennel broth 34
dandelion, ham hock 41–3
garlic, tomato sauce 37
green beans, chicken 27
honey, carrots 26
peppers, garlic 19, 24–5
spinach, Swiss chard 28–9
pastry dishes, courgettes,
    mint, ricotta 66–7
pea
    dill, Little Gem lettuce 64–5
    mint, dill 63
pear
    cinnamon, star anise 192–3
    lemon, rose sorbet 255
pepper, garlic, parsley 19, 24–5
pesto
    basil, garlic, pine nuts 1 50
    basil, garlic, pine nuts 2 50
pine nut
    basil, garlic 1 (pesto) 50
    basil, garlic 2 (pesto) 50
pineapple, banana, cinnamon
    bread 202–5
polenta, ricotta, lemon teacakes
    92–3
porcini
    barley, thyme soup 240–1
    tomato, ox cheek 234–9
pork
    bay, watercress 105–7
    cheek, coriander seed, barley
        218–21
porridge oats
    Bircher muesli 166–7
    muesli 168–71
potato
    aubergines, dill 58
    dill, capers 246–7

    fennel seed, garlic
        228–9
    lemon, oregano 80
prune
    bay, venison 122
    coriander seed, lamb
        222–3

R

radish, green leaves, dill
    70

raisin
  aubergine, mint 56–7
  Bircher muesli 166–7
  granola 172–3
  muesli 168–71
ramson, basil, lentil soup
  36
raspberry, meringues, cream,
  strawberry 150–1
red cabbage, caraway seed,
  apple 226–7
rhubarb, vanilla, custard
  144–7
ricotta
  courgettes, mint 66–7
  lemon, polenta teacakes
    92–3
rolled oats, granola 172–3
rose, lemon, pear sorbet 255
rose water, blood orange, mint
  257
rosemary
  bean, ham hock soup 123
  white bean, Swiss chard
    soup 108–9

S

sage
  garlic, beans 116–17
  lemon, veal chop 124–5
salads
  green leaves, dill, radish
    70–1
  ham hock, parsley, dandelion
    41–3
  kohlrabi, mint, smoked
    paprika 62
salad leaves, walnut dressing
  244

salami, courgettes, mint, ricotta
  66–7
salsa verde 250–4
salt 18
salt beef, bay, thyme 118–19
sauces
  berry, apple 122
  Mr Abraham's tomato 248
  tomato, parsley, garlic 37
schnitzels, chicken, parsley,
  breadcrumbs 38–40
sherry vinegar, dill, tomato
  60–1
smoked paprika, mint, kohlrabi
  62
smoothies, Josh's morning 141
sorbet
  banana, lemon 94
  pear, lemon, rose 255
soup
  barley, thyme, porcini 240–1
  borlotti, parsley, bread 47–9
  carrot, yoghurt, cumin
    159–61
  chestnut, nutmeg, bacon
    188–91
  chicken, parsley, carrot 32–3
  fennel broth, parsley, chicken
    34
  lentil, ramsons, basil 36
  Swiss chard, rosemary, white
    bean 108–9
spinach
  lemon, watercress 85
  salad leaves, walnut dressing
    244
  Swiss chard, parsley 28–9
star anise, cinnamon, pears
  192–3
stew
  aubergines, dill, potatoes
    58

lamb, coriander seed, prunes
  222–3
strawberry
  Josh's morning smoothie 141
  meringues, cream 150–1
sugar, cinnamon 88–91
Swiss chard
  parsley, spinach 28–9
  rosemary, white bean soup
    108–9

T

tarragon, lemon, chicken 81–3
teacakes, ricotta, lemon, polenta
  19, 92–3
thyme
  bay, salt beef 118–19
  porcini, barley soup 240–1
tomato
  borlotti, cinnamon 183
  cinnamon, garlic 182
  dill, sherry vinegar 60–1
  green beans, cinnamon
    184–5
  parsley, garlic sauce 37
  porcini, ox cheek 234–9
  sauce, Mr Abraham's 248
tomato juice, Josh's Virgin Mary
  208–11
tools 18
tzatziki 162–3

V

vanilla
  custard 142–3
  custard, rhubarb 144–7

meringues 1 148–9
yoghurt, apricots 165
yoghurt ice cream 164
veal
bay, carrots 112–14
chop, sage, lemon 124–5
venison, bay, prunes 122
Virgin Mary, Josh's 208–11

W

walnut
carrot, cinnamon cake
194–5
dressing, salad leaves 244
granola 172–3
watercress
bay, pork 105–7
green leaves, dill, radish
70–1
spinach, lemon 85

Y

yoghurt 156–7
apricots, vanilla 165
aubergine, lemon 158
Bircher muesli 166–7
cumin, carrot soup 159–61
ice cream 164
mint, cucumbers 162–3

It is an orchard never quite without fruit;
sometimes it just requires a little imagination.

Acknowledgements.

Without the following people this book would not have been possible . . .

Ruthie R. for giving me the opportunity to cook and promising me it would all be just fine!

Gordon P. for teaching me the ways of music and life.

Jonathan for being both the spring and succour in my step.

Siân W.O. and Joseph T. for taking a chance on me and giving me the confidence and support to change course, and for sharing with patience and generosity their know-how of Italian cooking - I learned from the best.

Lucy S. for keeping me on the straight and narrow.
Sarah J. for standing by my side for as long as it took. And for still standing there!
The entire team at Ebury, Sarah L., Caroline M. and Nick J. for believing in my potential.

I would also like to thank:

Andrew B.; Imogen F.; Andy S.; Laura F.; David E.;
Joanne H.; Isla M.P.; Greg M.; Amelia; J. Bagels;
Gerald M.; Frankie P.; Dylan M.; Mario M.; James F.;
Roberto C.; Tamas S.; Alex B.

10 9 8 7 6 5 4 3 2 1

Published in 2014 by Ebury Press, an imprint of Ebury Publishing
A Random House Group Company

Text © Natalia Conroy 2014

Photography © Andy Sewell 2014

Natalia Conroy has asserted her right to be identified as the author of this Work in
accordance with the Copyright, Designs and Patents Act 1988

The Random House Group Limited Reg. No. 954009

Addresses for companies within the Random House Group can be found at
www.randomhouse.co.uk

A CIP catalogue record for this book is available from the British Library

The Random House Group Limited supports the Forest Stewardship Council®
(FSC®), the leading international forest-certification organisation. Our books carrying
the FSC label are printed on FSC®-certified paper. FSC is the only forest-certification
scheme supported by the leading environmental organisations, including Greenpeace. Our
paper procurement policy can be found at www.randomhouse.co.uk/environment

To buy books by your favourite authors and register for offers visit www.randomhouse.co.uk

Design: Two Associates
Photography: Andy Sewell
Food and props stylist: Laura Fyfe

Colour origination by Altaimage, London
Printed and bound in China by C&C Offset Printing Co., Ltd

ISBN 9780091957582

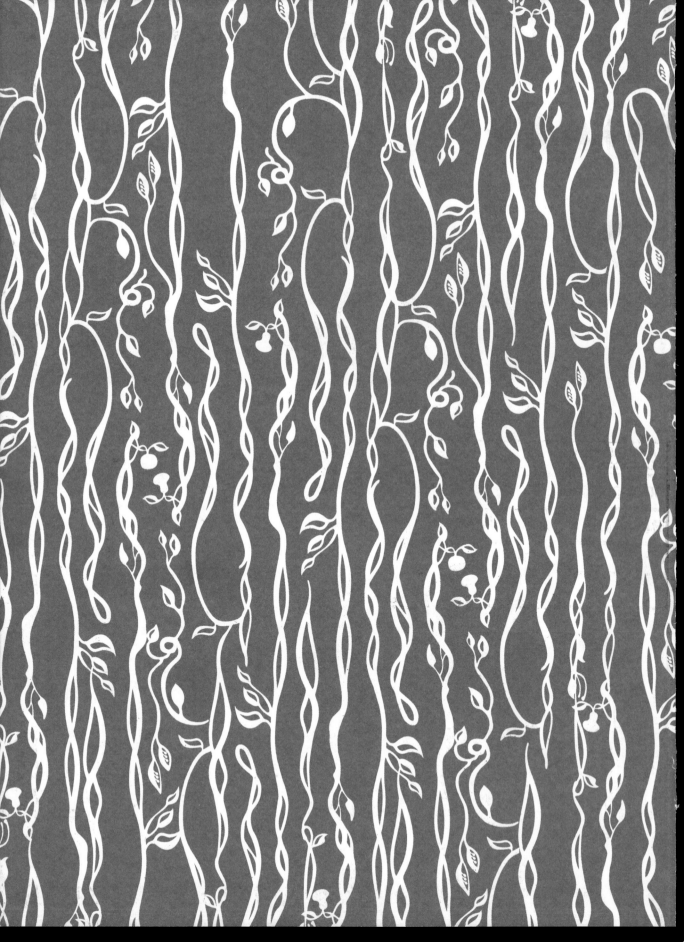